Step-by-Step Classic Kitchen

Poultry & Game

A hundred graded recipes with kitchen hints and wine guide

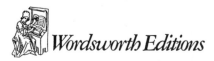

Wordsworth Editions

Step-by-Step Classic Kitchen

Poultry & Game

In recent years chickens have come to feature regularly in our family meals and are at the centre of many a dinner party, but all too often we seem to fall back on the same old way of preparing the bird for the table. Certainly a stuffed, roast chicken is delicious (and a specially tasty sausagemeat and spinach stuffing is described here) – but next time why not try roasting it *en pâte*, in a covering of flaky pastry? Or cooked with mushrooms in brown ale?

These are just some of the tempting and unusual recipes given in this book for one kind of chicken or another – poussin, roasting chicken, boiling fowl or cockerel – for in this country we tend to forget how important it is to choose the right bird for the right recipe. And (except for the traditional roast turkey and all the trimmings at Christmas) we overlook the other varieties of poultry there are available as well if we shop carefully around: guinea fowl, duck, and goose. All these, and rabbits and pigeons too, are included here.

The book tells you what to look for at the butchers when selecting your poultry, as well as giving detailed instructions for trussing or jointing your bird or rabbit. There is plenty of advice about garnishes, marinades, complementary side dishes and so on; and tips for barding and basting to ensure your roast fowl does not dry up.

We are sure you will enjoy experimenting with all the varied and exciting dishes described here, and the clear, step-by-step recipes will guarantee success every time. There is something here to suit every taste: firm favourites like *coq au vin* or rabbit with mustard sauce as well as luxurious dinner party dishes such as guinea fowl with cognac or chicken with crayfish. We hope you will go ahead and try them. Next year – who knows – perhaps you'll consider serving your Christmas turkey in a chocolate sauce. You'll find that here as well.

Table of Contents

Notes: Getting the Best out of this Book

1. The preparation times given in the Table of Contents and with each recipe are minimum times: they will vary according to the cook's ability and the equipment available. Certain of the recipes require periods for marinading or chilling. These have not been taken into account in the times given in the table, but are indicated at the head of each recipe.

2. It is best to use double cream for most recipes – it is the nearest equivalent to French cream. Remember also that the French use unsalted butter, and this is assumed in the recipes unless otherwise stated.

3. It is always best to use red or white wine vinegar in the recipes where vinegar is required; the results will not be the same if you use malt vinegar. In the same way, freshly ground black pepper should always be used in preference to ready-ground pepper.

4. Oven temperatures. The following are Gas, Fahrenheit and Centigrade equivalents:

Gas	¼	½	1	2	3	4	5	6	7	8	9
°F	225	250	275	300	325	350	375	400	425	450	475
°C	110	120	140	160	170	180	190	200	220	230	250

5. It is important when using these recipes to follow the exact proportions. A set of kitchen scales, measuring jug, glass and spoons are essential. Follow either metric *or* avoirdupois measurements in each recipe.

6. To help you choose the right wine for your meal, see page 80.

Coquelets aux Trois Poivrons

Serves 6. Preparation: 20 min Cooking: 1 hr

Poussins with Three Peppers

★★

○ **3 good-sized poussins**
○ **3 thin slices smoked streaky bacon**
○ **60ml (4 tbls) olive oil**
○ **2 cloves garlic**
○ **2 medium-sized onions**
○ **45ml (3 tbls) brandy**
○ **1 green pepper**
○ **1 yellow pepper**
○ **1 red pepper**
○ **500g (18 oz) ripe tomatoes**
○ **salt and pepper**

1. Peel and chop the garlic finely. Peel the onions and cut into thin slices.
2. Wash the peppers and cut them into halves. Remove the seeds, then cut into strips 2cm (¾ inch) thick and dice them.
3. Scald the tomatoes in boiling water for 30 seconds, refresh under cold running water, then peel and cut into halves. Squeeze to extract the seeds and chop the tomato pulp roughly.
4. Chop the bacon into small pieces.
5. Heat the oil in a flameproof casserole over a moderate heat and brown the poussins on both sides for about 10 minutes. Pour in the brandy and set alight.
6. Add the bacon, onion, garlic and peppers. Brown over a low heat for 10 minutes, making sure they do not burn, then add the chopped tomato. Season. Cover the casserole and cook for a further 30 minutes over a very low heat. Turn the poussins frequently. Remove the lid and continue cooking for 5 minutes to reduce the sauce until it is a thick consistency.
7. Place the poussins on a serving dish, spoon the peppers around and serve immediately.

Capon au Kirsch

Serves 6. Preparation: 15 min Cooking: 1 hr 45 min

Capon with Kirsch

○ **1 2kg (4½ lb) capon, cut into 20 pieces**
○ **90ml (6 tbls) oil**
○ **100g (4 oz) smoked bacon**
○ **2 medium-sized onions**
○ **100g (4 oz) button mushrooms**
○ **10 sprigs parsley**
○ **2 bay leaves**
○ **125g (5 oz) double cream**
○ **200ml (7 fl oz) dry white wine**
○ **5ml (1 tsp) cornflour**
○ **30ml (2 tbls) water**
○ **1 small bunch chives**
○ **45ml (3 tbls) Kirsch**
○ **salt and pepper**

1. Cut the bacon into strips. Chop the parsley roughly. Cut off the mushroom stalks, wash and drain. Peel and finely slice the onions.
2. Heat the oil in a flameproof casserole and brown the capon joints and bacon over a high heat, turning frequently. Add the sliced onions, bay leaves and wine and season. Cover the casserole and cook over a low heat for 45 minutes.
3. Slice the mushrooms thinly and add to the ingredients in the casserole, together with the parsley. Cook over a very low heat for a further 45 minutes, turning the capon pieces frequently. Then remove the capon pieces and keep warm in the oven.
4. Mix the cornflour with the cold water and add to the cream. Blend the mixture into the casserole and leave to boil for 2 minutes, until the sauce thickens.
5. Chop the chives roughly, add to the sauce and put the capon pieces back in the casserole. Turn the heat off, pour in the Kirsch, and serve immediately.

Serve with fresh buttered pasta or seasonal vegetables.

A capon is a young cockerel (7 to 10 months old) which is neutered and fattened like a large roaster. Its flesh is firm, tasty and less fatty than that of the large roaster. It can weigh up to 3kg (6½ lb).

Coquelets aux Trois Poivrons ▶

Escalopes de Poulet Panées

Serves 4. Preparation: 15 min Cooking: 20 min

Chicken Escalopes

★★

- ○ **4 chicken breasts**
- ○ **1 egg**
- ○ **30ml (2 tbls) double cream**
- ○ **salt, pepper and nutmeg**
- ○ **6 slices white bread**
- ○ **oil for frying**

1. Preheat the oven to 180°C (350°F; gas mark 4). Cut the crusts off the bread, put the slices on a baking tray and toast in the oven for 10 minutes. Leave to cool. When cool, crush with a rolling pin to obtain breadcrumbs and put in a bowl.
2. Beat the egg in a bowl and add the cream, salt, pepper and grated nutmeg. Blend all the ingredients together with a fork.
3. Cut each chicken breast into two slices and flatten them out with the blade of a knife.
4. Dip each escalope of chicken into the egg mixture and coat with the breadcrumbs.
5. Heat 100ml (3½ fl oz) of oil in a frying pan over a low heat. Fry the escalopes for 5 minutes, turning once, and drain on kitchen paper.

Garnish with lemon wedges, or, if you wish, with knobs of butter *maître d'hôtel*.

Serve with a green salad, mixed salad or corn salad etc.

To prepare butter *maître d'hôtel*, cream 50g (2 oz) of unsalted butter with 30ml (2 tbls) of lemon juice and 15ml (1 tbls) of finely chopped parsley. Season.

Poularde à la Flamande

Serves 6. Preparation: 15 min Cooking: 1 hr 45 min

Chicken Flemish-Style

★★

- ○ **1 1.6kg (3½ lb) boiling fowl, trussed**
- ○ **1 carrot**
- ○ **3 leeks (the white part only)**
- ○ **2 celery stalks**
- ○ **1 onion**
- ○ **50g (2 oz) butter**
- ○ **1 bouquet garni: 1 bay leaf, 4 sprigs of parsley, 1 sprig of thyme**
- ○ **2 egg yolks**
- ○ **125g (5 oz) double cream**
- ○ **300g (11 oz) long-grain rice**
- ○ **salt and pepper**

1. Wash the vegetables and cut into thin strips. Melt the butter in a flameproof casserole large enough to contain the fowl. Gently sauté the vegetables over a low heat for 5 to 6 minutes, but do not let them brown.
2. Put the fowl in the casserole, pour over enough cold water to cover it and add the bouquet garni. Season. Cover the casserole and cook over a low heat for 1 hour 15 minutes.
3. After 1 hour cook the rice in a large quantity of salted, boiling water. Drain and keep warm in a covered saucepan.
4. Remove the fowl from the casserole. Check that the meat is tender and well cooked by pricking the thigh with a fork. If undercooked return to the casserole and cook for a little longer. When cooked, place on a serving dish and keep warm.
5. Reduce the cooking liquid by boiling over a high heat until you are left with approximately ¾ litre (1 pint). Meanwhile, remove the skin from the fowl. Cut the fowl into pieces, put the rice on a serving dish and arrange the pieces on top. Keep warm in the oven, having first covered the dish with foil.
6. When the cooking liquid has reduced, mix the eggs with the cream; remove the casserole from the heat and slowly pour in the egg/cream mixture. Beat with a whisk for 2 minutes.
7. Pour the sauce over the chicken and rice and serve immediately.

Poulet Rôti Farci

Roast Chicken with Basic Stuffing

Serves 6. Preparation: 30 min Cooking: 1 hr 30 min

★★★

- ○ 1 chicken, about 1.8kg (4 lb)
- ○ 15ml (1 tbls) oil
- ○ 4 slices white bread
- ○ 100ml (3½ fl oz) boiling milk
- ○ 3 finely chopped shallots
- ○ 100g (4 oz) pork sausagemeat
- ○ 100g (4 oz) minced, cooked ham
- ○ the chicken liver
- ○ 200g (7 oz) frozen spinach, cooked and drained
- ○ 30ml (2 tbls) finely chopped herbs or parsley
- ○ 1 egg
- ○ salt, pepper and nutmeg
- ○ *quatre épices* or mixed spice
- ○ 20g (¾ oz) butter

1. Cut the crusts off the bread, dip in the boiling milk, then place in a bowl and mash with a fork.
2. Put the butter in a small frying pan, add the shallots and sauté over a low heat. Then add the sausagemeat and fry gently, mashing it up with a fork. Pour the sausage and onion into a bowl and add the minced ham.
3. Chop the spinach and add to the ingredients in the bowl together with the herbs. Season to taste with salt, pepper and grated nutmeg. Sprinkle with a pinch of *quatre épices* and mix well.
4. Dice the liver and add to the stuffing. Add the egg and mix it in well with a fork.
5. Fill the chicken with the stuffing and sew up the vent with a trussing needle and a strong piece of string.
6. Preheat the oven to 220°C (425°F; gas mark 7). Brush the chicken with oil and place in a roasting tin. Place in the centre of the oven, reduce the oven to 200°C (400°F; gas mark 6) and roast for 30 minutes. Then reduce to 190°C (375°F; gas mark 5) and cook for a further 30 minutes. Reduce the oven once more to 180°C (350°F; gas mark 4) and cook for 30 minutes more. Add a little water from time to time if it looks as if the chicken is drying out. After 1 hour 30 minutes check if the chicken is done by pricking the leg with a fork: the juices should run clear yellow.
7. Place the chicken on a serving dish. Carve, and cut the stuffing into slices. Serve the cooking liquid separately in a sauceboat.

A few suggestions for vegetables to serve with roast chicken: puréed vegetables either individually or mixed, such as carrots, celery, turnip, cauliflower, courgettes or green peas, depending on the time of year.

Fricassée de Poulet au Citron

Chicken Fricassée with Lemon

Serves 6. Preparation: 15 min Cooking: 1 hr

★

- ○ 1 1.6kg (3½ lb) chicken, cut into 12 pieces
- ○ 1 large onion
- ○ 80g (3 oz) butter
- ○ 15ml (1 tbls) flour
- ○ 1 chicken stock cube
- ○ ½ litre (18 fl oz) hot water
- ○ 250g (9 oz) cream
- ○ 2 egg yolks
- ○ 2 lemons
- ○ salt and pepper

1. Peel the onion and cut into thin slices.
2. Melt the butter in a flameproof casserole over a low heat. Gently sauté the onion and chicken joints, sprinkle in the flour and blend well in.
3. Dissolve the stock cube in hot water and pour over the chicken pieces. Cover and simmer for 45 minutes, turning the meat occasionally.
4. Squeeze the juice from the lemons and add it to the cream and egg yolks, beating with a fork. Pour into the casserole and stir rapidly for 30 seconds. Check the seasoning, add some freshly ground pepper and serve at once.

Serve with boiled rice, dried in the oven.

Before you cook most kinds of meat cut off the fat first.

To make canapés, and for certain recipes which require bread, cut the crusts off the bread first.

Poulet au Genièvre

Serves 4. Preparation: 5 min Cooking: 1 hr

Chicken with Juniper Berries

★★

○ 1 1.2kg (2½ lb) chicken, cut into 8 pieces
○ 10 finely chopped shallots
○ 60g (2½ oz) butter
○ 200ml (7 fl oz) dry white wine
○ 20 juniper berries
○ 5ml (1 tsp) cornflour
○ 30ml (2 tbls) cold water
○ 200g (7 oz) cream
○ salt and pepper

1. Melt the butter in a frying pan and sauté the chicken pieces, turning them with a spatula. Add the shallots and cook until it is all golden brown. This must be done over a low heat to prevent the shallots burning.
2. Add the wine and juniper berries. Season. Cover the pan and simmer for 35 minutes.
3. Remove the chicken pieces and keep warm on a serving dish.
4. Reduce the cooking juices to 30ml (2 tbls) over a high heat.
5. Mix the cornflour with the cold water and add to the cream. Pour into the frying pan and boil for 2 minutes, then pour over the chicken pieces and serve at once.

Serve with sauté potatoes.

Curry de Poulet

Serves 6. Preparation: 10 min Cooking: 1 hr 10 min

Curried Chicken

○ 1 1.6kg (3½ lb) chicken, cut into 12 pieces
○ 300g (11 oz) onions
○ 60ml (4 tbls) oil
○ 1 cooking apple
○ 1 unripe banana
○ 60ml (4 tbls) curry powder
○ 15ml (1 tbls) flour
○ 100g (4 oz) cream or natural yoghurt
○ ½ lemon
○ salt
○ ¼ litre (9 fl oz) milk
○ 70g (3 oz) grated coconut

1. Bring the milk to the boil in a saucepan and sprinkle in the grated coconut. Turn the heat off and cover the saucepan. Leave to soak. Peel the onions and cut into thin slices.
2. Heat the oil in a flameproof casserole, brown the chicken pieces on both sides and reserve. Put the onions in the casserole and gently sauté until they become transparent.
3. Peel the apple and banana and grate them. Add to the casserole, and once they have taken on a golden brown colour sprinkle in the flour and the curry powder. Then add the coconut and milk mixture, passing it through a sieve; squeeze well to extract all the milk. You can substitute an equal amount of water for this if you wish.
4. Put the chicken pieces back into the casserole. Season and cover with a lid. Simmer for 45 minutes, turning the meat occasionally. Check to make sure the sauce does not burn.
5. 5 minutes before the end of the cooking time add the cream or yoghurt. Then remove the chicken pieces and place on a serving dish. Keep warm.
6. Add the juice of ½ a lemon to the sauce and liquidize it (or pass it through a fine meshed sieve) to obtain a creamy sauce. Pour over the chicken pieces.

Curried chicken may be served with boiled rice (dried slightly in a warm oven), slices of banana with lemon juice, fresh pineapple cut into cubes, diced fresh mangoes, and slices of cucumber mixed with natural yoghurt that has been salted and flavoured with chopped mint.

To bard a chicken is to cover the breast with thin sheets of pork fat (the best type is back fat) or with rashers of streaky bacon. This is necessary to prevent the meat becoming too dry when roasting.

Coquelets aux Olives

Serves 6. Preparation: 15 min Cooking: 1 hr

Braised Poussins with Olives

★★

○ **3 poussins**
○ **60g (2½ oz) thin slices of streaky bacon**
○ **60ml (4 tbls) oil**
○ **50g (2 oz) butter**
○ **30ml (2 tbls) anchovy paste**
○ **1 small tin 400g (14 oz) tomatoes**
○ **2ml (½ tsp) oregano**
○ **1 small chilli (or some cayenne pepper)**
○ **150g (6 oz) stoned black olives**
○ **30ml (2 tbls) capers**
○ **15ml (1 tbls) chopped parsley, or fresh chopped basil, or chopped chives**

1. Peel and finely chop the onion. Chop the bacon into small pieces and slice the olives. Drain the capers.
2. Remove the seeds from the tinned tomatoes. Mash roughly with a fork and put into a bowl with the juice.
3. Heat the oil in a large flameproof casserole over a medium heat. Add the onion and bacon and sauté for 5 minutes, then add the butter and brown the poussins on both sides for 10 minutes.
4. Put the anchovy paste into the casserole and blend well with the cooking juices. Turn the poussins in the sauce for two minutes. Then add the tomatoes, oregano, chopped chilli (or cayenne pepper) and cover the casserole. Simmer for 40 minutes, turning the poussins occasionally.
5. Add the capers and olives 10 minutes before the end of the cooking time.
6. When the poussins are cooked place on a serving dish and pour the sauce over them. Sprinkle with herbs and serve at once.

Serve with slices of bread, toasted and rubbed with garlic.

Poulet à l'Ail Nouveau

Serves 4. Preparation: 15 min Cooking: 55 min

Chicken with Fresh Garlic

★★

○ **1 1.2kg (2½ lb) chicken, cut into 8 pieces**
○ **50g (2 oz) butter**
○ **15ml (1 tbls) oil**
○ **salt and pepper**
○ **2 heads of fresh garlic, finely chopped**
○ **100ml (3½ fl oz) dry white wine**
○ **½ litre (18 fl oz) warm milk**
○ **5ml (1 tsp) cornflour**
○ **30ml (2 tbls) cold water**
○ **60ml (4 tbls) cream**

1. Heat the oil in a flameproof casserole over a low heat. Add half the butter and brown the chicken pieces on both sides. Season. Remove from the casserole and reserve.
2. Pour off the cooking fat from the casserole and put in the remaining butter and the garlic. Stir continuously with a spatula until it has a creamy consistency. Then pour in the wine and put the chicken pieces back into the casserole. Stir well until the wine has completely evaporated.
3. Pour in the milk and cover the casserole. Simmer for 30 minutes.
4. Remove the chicken and place on a serving dish. Keep warm.
5. Mix the cornflour with the cold water. Blend with the cream and pour into the casserole. Boil the sauce for 2 minutes over a high heat, stirring continuously, then strain through a sieve and pour over the chicken pieces.

Serve with small potato cakes or potato croquettes.

Pork sausagemeat in France is known as chair à saucisse, *which is simply pure pork and pork fat minced and seasoned with salt, pepper and herbs. The best substitute in England is fresh, fairly fat pork, minced and well seasoned.*

Poulet au Sel
Chicken Baked in Salt

Serves 4. Preparation: 10 min Cooking: 1 hr 30 min

★★

- ○ 1 1.5kg (3½ lb) chicken
- ○ 1 sprig of tarragon
- ○ 10 green peppercorns
- ○ 4kg (9 lb) coarse sea salt

1. Preheat the oven to its maximum setting. Place the peppercorns and the tarragon inside the chicken. Truss the chicken; make sure the neck skin is held in place by the wing tips and that the vent is firmly closed with a skewer or sewn up to prevent the salt getting inside the chicken.
2. Line the bottom and sides of an ovenproof dish, large enough to hold the chicken, with a sheet of foil. Pour 1kg (2¼ lb) of salt into the dish. Spread out well to cover the bottom completely. Place the chicken on top, breast downwards. Pour the remaining salt around and over the chicken. It should be covered by a layer at least 2cm (1 inch) thick.
3. Place the dish, uncovered, in the hot oven for 1 hour 30 minutes.
4. Remove from the oven very carefully, as the dish will be extremely hot. Turn on to a serving dish and remove the foil. The chicken and salt will have formed a solid block.
5. Place the serving dish on the table and break open the salt with a small hammer in front of your guests: the chicken will appear, golden and crusty, tasting delicious.

For this recipe to be a success it is best to use a top-quality fresh chicken.

Tajine de Poulet
Chicken Moroccan-Style

Serves 4. Preparation: 10 min Cooking: 1 hr 30 min

★★

- ○ 1 1.6kg (3½ lb) chicken, cut into 8 pieces
- ○ 2 medium-sized onions
- ○ 1 pinch of saffron
- ○ 5ml (1 tsp) powdered ginger
- ○ 150ml (5 fl oz) oil
- ○ ¼ litre (9 fl oz) water
- ○ 10 sprigs of parsley
- ○ 20 sprigs of coriander
- ○ 5ml (1 tsp) red pepper
- ○ 2.5ml (½ tsp) cumin
- ○ 30ml (2 tbls) lemon juice
- ○ 24 stoned green olives
- ○ 1 pickled lemon
- ○ salt

1. Peel and finely chop the onions. Place in a casserole and add the ginger, saffron, oil and water. Mix well.
2. Place the chicken pieces in the casserole and turn them in the mixture of spices until they are well coated. Add a little more water if necessary and season with salt. Cover and cook for approximately 1 hour 15 minutes, or until the chicken flesh is tender and comes away from the bone easily. While cooking baste the chicken pieces with the sauce so that the meat is well flavoured by the spices.
3. Meanwhile, wash the parsley and coriander. Dry and chop the leaves.
4. 15 minutes before the end of the cooking time add the red pepper, cumin, chopped parsley and coriander to the casserole. Stir well.
5. When the chicken is cooked, dice the pickled lemon and add to the casserole together with the olives and lemon juice. Mix well. Reduce the sauce, with the casserole uncovered, until it is thick and creamy.
6. Pour into a serving dish and serve immediately.

If you cannot get hold of a pickled lemon for this Moroccan recipe, grate the peel of a fresh lemon into the casserole. Pickled lemons or *citrons confits* are small lemons with a strong flavour, preserved in brine.

Coquelets à l'Orange

Serves 6. Preparation: 5 min Cooking: 50 min

Roast Poussins with Orange Sauce

★

- ○ **3 poussins**
- ○ **6 oranges (blood oranges are the best)**
- ○ **150ml (5 fl oz) dry white wine**
- ○ **60ml (4 tbls) cognac**
- ○ **salt and pepper**
- ○ **60g (2½ oz) butter**
- ○ **30ml (2 tbls) oil**

1. Preheat the oven to 220°C (425°F; gas mark 7).
2. Cut a strip 9cm (3½ inches) long from the peel of one of the oranges. Cut it into three more pieces. Brush the poussins with oil. Rub inside and outside with salt and pepper. Place a knob of butter (20g/¾ oz) inside each poussin, together with one strip of orange peel, the liver, heart and gizzard.
3. Grease an ovenproof dish and place the poussins on it. Brown in the oven for 15 minutes. Then pour the wine over them and, when it has evaporated, add 30ml (2 tbls) of cognac. Cook for a further 30 minutes.
4. Squeeze 3 oranges; peel the remaining three and cut into thin slices.
5. When the poussins are cooked place on a serving dish. Pour the remainder of the cognac into the cooking dish and add the orange juice. Reduce the sauce by half and pour it over the poussins.
6. Garnish with the orange slices and serve immediately.

Blancs de Poulet aux Petits Oignons

*Serves 4. Preparation: 10 min
Cooking: 50 min*

Braised Chicken Breasts with Small Onions

★ ★

- ○ **4 chicken breasts**
- ○ **salt, pepper and nutmeg**
- ○ **8 leaves of fresh sage**
- ○ **60g (3 oz) butter**
- ○ **2 bunches of spring onions (or pickling onions)**
- ○ **1 bay leaf**
- ○ **1 sprig of thyme**
- ○ **1 clove**
- ○ **½ litre (1 pint) milk**

1. Trim the roots of the onions. Peel, wash and wipe them dry. Melt the butter in a casserole over a low heat. Gently sauté the onions, turning them frequently, for approximately 20 minutes.
2. Cut each chicken breast into 2 slices and season with salt, pepper and grated nutmeg. Place a sage leaf at one end of each breast and roll it up like a cigar. Secure each roll with a toothpick or cocktail stick.
3. Bring the milk to the boil together with the bay leaf, thyme, clove, salt and pepper. Turn the heat down and simmer for 10 minutes.
4. After the onions have been cooking for 20 minutes add the chicken rolls and brown lightly. Then sieve the hot milk and add to the casserole.
5. Cover the casserole and simmer over a low heat for 25 minutes, stirring from time to time. When cooked, the sauce should be thick and golden. If not, reduce the sauce a little longer in the uncovered casserole. Serve very hot.

For a more filling meal serve with small potato cakes or sauté potatoes.

When serving poultry make sure that the serving dish, sauceboat and plates have been warmed in the oven. If possible use a plate warmer to keep the serving dish hot during the meal. Otherwise poultry tends to lose its flavour.

Jambonneaux de Poulet aux Cèpes

Stuffed Chicken Legs with Mushrooms

Serves 4.
Preparation: 20 min Cooking: 45 min
★ ★ ★

○ **4 large chicken legs**
○ **1 chicken breast**
○ **100g (4 oz) pork sausagemeat**
○ **100g (4 oz) Gruyère cheese**
○ **10 sprigs parsley**
○ **1 egg**
○ **salt and pepper**
○ **pinch nutmeg**
○ **50g (2 oz) unsmoked bacon**
○ **1 medium-sized onion**
○ **400g (14 oz) mushrooms**
○ **50g (2 oz) butter**
○ **30ml (2 tbls) groundnut oil**
○ **100ml (3½ fl oz) dry white wine**
○ **5 sprigs parsley**
○ **5 sprigs chervil**
○ **1 sprig tarragon**
○ **10 chives**

1. Bone the chicken legs, using a sharp knife and keeping the skin intact. Cut the chicken breast into thin strips, then dice. Grate the cheese and chop the parsley.
2. Place the diced chicken breast, sausagemeat, cheese and parsley in a bowl. Break in an egg. Season with salt, pepper and grated nutmeg. Mix all the ingredients together well, using a fork.
3. Divide into 4 and fill each leg with the stuffing, pushing it in. Sew up the skin with a needle and thread. They should look like knuckle joints of ham.
4. Cut the bacon into strips approximately 0.5cm (¼ inch). Peel and chop the onion finely. Take off the mushroom stalks; wash and slice.
5. Pour the oil and butter into a frying pan. Gently fry the chicken legs for 10 minutes, turning occasionally. Remove from heat. Then brown the onion and bacon lightly in the pan. Add the mushrooms and gently fry for 5 minutes more or until their juices have begun to run. Put the chicken legs back into the pan.
6. Preheat the oven to 200°C (400°F; gas mark 6). Pour the contents of the pan into an ovenproof dish. Pour in the wine and cook in the oven for 30 minutes; turn the chicken legs once and baste twice with the cooking juices.
7. Meanwhile, prepare the herbs: wash, wipe dry and strip off the stalks. Finely chop the leaves. When the meat is cooked remove the dish from the oven and sprinkle with the chopped herbs.

Serve at once with sautéed potatoes or polenta.

Poule au Pot

Chicken in the Pot

Serves 6. Preparation: 10 min Cooking: 2 hr 15 min
★ ★

○ **1 2½kg (4½-5 lb) boiling fowl**
○ **6 carrots**
○ **3 turnips**
○ **3 leeks**
○ **1 celery heart**
○ **1 medium-sized onion**
○ **3 cloves**
○ **salt**

Bouquet garni:
○ **1 sprig thyme**
○ **1 bay leaf**
○ **4 sprigs parsley**

1. Peel and wash the vegetables.
2. Spike the onion with the cloves. Tie the leeks in a bunch. Tie the herbs together to make the bouquet garni.
3. Place the chicken in a large saucepan. Cover with cold water. Bring to the boil over a medium heat. Skim when necessary.
4. Season with salt. Add the vegetables and bouquet garni.
5. Boil slowly for 2 hours. Then remove the chicken and carve. Serve surrounded by the vegetables.

The gravy should be served separately. Accompany with coarse sea salt and small gherkins.

Polenta, either yellow or white, makes a delicious accompaniment to any roast or meat dish with a sauce. Corn meal made from dried, ground maize, polenta is easy to cook: just boil it in milk or stock and serve at once. Or leave it to cool and then cut into shapes (squares, rectangles, triangles etc) and cook au gratin, ie in the oven with butter and cheese. These small dumplings are known as gnocchi.

Poularde à la Farce Blanche
Braised Chicken with White Stuffing

Serves 6. Preparation: 20-40 min
Cooking: 1 hr 45 min
★ ★ ★

- ○ 1 large 1.5kg (3¼ lb) pullet
- ○ 2 chicken breasts
- ○ 1 veal sweetbread
- ○ 80g (3 oz) double cream
- ○ 1 egg white
- ○ salt and white pepper
- ○ 200g (7 oz) barding fat (thin slices of pork fat)
- ○ 50g (2 oz) butter
- ○ 100g (4 oz) raw ham
- ○ 24 small onions (or pickling onions)
- ○ 30ml (2 tbls) cognac
- ○ 30ml (2 tbls) Liqueur de Vervaine

1. Have the chicken boned by your butcher, if possible. If you want to bone it yourself, make a cut down the centre of the back, using a sharp knife. Then cut the flesh away from the bones. You can remove the lower part of the wings, the feet and lower leg, or leave them attached, as you wish.
2. Poach the sweetbread in simmering water with vinegar added for 5 minutes. Drain and dice. Chop the raw chicken breasts with a sharp knife. Dice the ham and peel the onions.
3. Mix the ingredients for the stuffing in a bowl: chicken breasts, sweetbread, cream, egg white, salt and white pepper. Stuff the chicken and truss it. Bard it by covering with slices of the pork fat and securing with string.
4. Melt the butter in a large flameproof casserole and brown the chicken on all sides. Add the diced ham. Season with pepper and a little salt. Add 2 tablespoons of water. Cover the casserole and simmer over a low heat for 30 minutes; turn the chicken frequently, and add a little water when necessary.
5. After 30 minutes, add the onions to the casserole and continue cooking for a further 30 minutes. Then remove the chicken from the casserole. Discard the string and barding fat and put the chicken back into the casserole. Continue to cook over a low heat for another 30 minutes, turning frequently so that it browns on all sides.
6. When cooked pour the cognac and Liqueur de Vervaine into the casserole. Simmer for 2 minutes, turning the chicken all the time in the sauce. Add a little water to deglaze the sauce, scraping up the cooking juices from the bottom of the pan.
7. Place the chicken on a serving dish and surround with the onions. Pour the sauce over the chicken and serve at once.

The Liqueur de Vervaine may be omitted if it is not available.

Blancs de Poulet à la Cannelle
Fried Chicken Breasts with Cinnamon

Serves 4. Preparation: 5 min Cooking: 25 min
★

- ○ 4 chicken breasts
- ○ 30ml (2 tbls) flour
- ○ 50g (2 oz) butter
- ○ 1 medium-sized onion
- ○ salt and pepper
- ○ 2ml (½ tsp) cinnamon
- ○ 2 cloves
- ○ 100ml (3½ fl oz) white wine vinegar
- ○ 60ml (4 tbls) double cream

1. Peel and finely chop the onion.
2. Cut each chicken breast into two. Flatten them with the blade of a knife.
3. Sprinkle a little flour onto each slice.
4. Melt the butter in a frying pan. Add the onion and chicken and brown lightly over a medium heat.
5. Then add the vinegar, cloves, cinnamon, salt and pepper. When the vinegar has completely evaporated pour in the cream. Cover the frying pan.
6. Simmer over a low heat for 15 minutes turning from time to time with a spatula.

Serve with sautéed vegetables: carrots, turnips, celery hearts.

A pullet is a young bird (5½ to 9 months old) which has not laid eggs. Its flesh is slightly fattier than that of a chicken and is therefore suitable for poaching; but you may stuff and roast it in the oven, or cook it in a casserole.

Coquelets Farcis à la Broche
Stuffed and Spit-Roasted Poussins

Serves 4. Preparation: 25 min Cooking: 40 min

★★

- ○ **2 poussins**
- ○ **300g (11 oz) lean minced pork**
- ○ **30ml (2 tbls) oil**
- ○ **1 large onion, finely chopped**
- ○ **1 egg**
- ○ **salt and pepper**
- ○ **pinch nutmeg**
- ○ **1 rasher 1.5cm (½ inch) thick smoked bacon**

1. Heat the oil in a frying pan. Gently fry the onion, then add the minced pork and brown over a low heat for 10 minutes. Transfer the contents of the frying pan to a bowl. Add the egg, season with salt, pepper and grated nutmeg. Mix well.
2. Divide the mixture into two and stuff each poussin. Sew the vent of each bird with a needle and thread.
3. Cut the bacon rasher into 6 pieces.
4. Thread onto a spit: two pieces of bacon, a poussin, two more pieces of bacon, the other poussin, and finish with the last two pieces of bacon.
5. Cook in the oven for 40 minutes, turning the spit from time to time.

Serve on a bed of buttered spinach.

Coq en Pâte
Cockerel Baked in Pastry

Serves 6. Preparation: 30 min Cooking: 1 hr 10 min

 ★★★

- ○ **1 1.5kg (3¼ lb) cockerel**
- ○ **4 shallots**
- ○ **4 sprigs parsley**
- ○ **the liver of the bird**
- ○ **100g (4 oz) chicken livers**
- ○ **30ml (2 tbls) brandy**
- ○ **2 eggs**
- ○ **80g (3 oz) butter**
- ○ **salt and pepper**
- ○ **500g (18 oz) frozen puff pastry**

1. Prepare the puff pastry, following the instructions on the packet.
2. Peel and finely chop the shallots. Wash the parsley, remove the stalks, and chop coarsely. Dice the livers. Beat one of the eggs well in a bowl.
3. In a frying pan melt 30g (1 oz) of butter. Gently fry the shallots and then brown the chopped livers. Pour in the beaten egg and brandy. Mix vigorously and remove from the heat. Add the chopped parsley and stuff the cockerel with this mixture.
4. Sew the vent of the bird with a needle and thread, and truss it, to secure the wings and legs.
5. Melt the remaining butter in a flameproof casserole. Brown the cockerel on all sides. Season. Remove from heat.
6. Preheat the oven to 220°C (425°F; gas mark 7). Grease a baking tray.
7. Divide the puff pastry into two pieces: one ⅓, the other ⅔. Roll out the smaller piece to a thickness of 0.5cm (¼ inch). Place on the greased baking tray and put the cockerel on top. Roll out the larger piece of puff pastry to the same thickness. Place over the cockerel and wet the edges. Seal the two pieces together using your fingertips.
8. Beat the other egg in a bowl and brush the pastry with it. Make a hole in the top and insert a rolled piece of greaseproof paper. This is to allow the steam to escape. Cook in the oven for 1 hour.
9. Serve at once. Carve at the table.

If you spit-roast a chicken, you should choose one with a good amount of fat. The fat will melt in the heat of cooking, and its flesh will be less dry. If you oven roast a chicken it is best to use one that is less fatty so that it does not swim in its own grease. But this does not necessarily mean one that is small.

Coquelets aux Légumes Nouveaux
Poussins with New Vegetables

Serves 4. Preparation: 15 min
Cooking: 50 min
★

- ○ **2 poussins**
- ○ **150g (6 oz) butter**
- ○ **1 bunch of spring onions**
- ○ **500g (1 lb 2 oz) new carrots**
- ○ **15ml (1 tbls) sugar**
- ○ **500g (1 lb 2 oz) new potatoes**
- ○ **3 sprigs tarragon**
- ○ **salt and pepper**

1. Rub the inside of the poussins with salt and pepper. Place a sprig of tarragon inside each bird.
2. Peel the onions, carrots and potatoes. Wash them. Drain and wipe the onions and carrots. Place the potatoes in a saucepan and cover with cold water. Cut the carrots in slices 1cm (½ inch) thick.
3. Melt 50g (2 oz) of butter in a flameproof casserole and brown the poussins all over, over a low heat, for 15 minutes. Continue cooking for a further 25 minutes, adding 30ml (2 tbls) water each time the sauce starts to caramelize. Season.
4. Meanwhile, prepare the vegetables. Boil the potatoes over a medium heat for about 15 minutes. Melt 50g (2 oz) of butter in a saucepan and lightly brown the onions and carrots. Season with salt and sprinkle with sugar. When the sugar has taken on a golden colour, add 200ml (7 fl oz) of water and simmer for about 20 minutes. When cooked, there should be no liquid left in the saucepan.
5. When the potatoes are cooked, strain off the water and replace on the heat with the remaining butter. Season with salt. Brown the potatoes, then sprinkle with the chopped tarragon leaves.
6. When the poussins are cooked, place on a serving dish, and surround with the vegetables. Serve at once.

Coquelets Fantaisie
Roast Poussins with Vegetables and Vermouth

Serves 4. Preparation: 15 min Cooking: 1 hr
★★

- ○ **2 poussins**
- ○ **60ml (4 tbls) oil**
- ○ **2 medium-sized onions**
- ○ **100g (4 oz) smoked streaky bacon**
- ○ **500g (1 lb 2 oz) small new potatoes**
- ○ **100g (4 oz) stoneless green olives**
- ○ **250g (9 oz) button mushrooms**
- ○ **4 ripe tomatoes**
- ○ **salt and pepper**
- ○ **150ml (5 fl oz) dry white vermouth**

1. Rub the inside of the poussins with salt and pepper. Brush them with 15ml (1 tbls) of oil. Season the outside with salt.
2. Preheat the oven to 200°C (400°F; gas mark 6). Cut the bacon into strips.
3. Peel and finely slice the onions. Trim the mushrooms and quarter. Peel the potatoes. Wash and wipe them dry.
4. Pour 45ml (3 tbls) of oil into a frying pan. Add the sliced onions, bacon strips and potatoes. Brown all the ingredients for 10 minutes, then add the mushrooms and olives. Season with salt and pepper. Simmer for 5 minutes and then pour all the ingredients into an ovenproof dish.
5. Place the poussins on top. Cut the tomatoes in half and place around the poussins. Pour in the vermouth and cook in the oven for 45 minutes, basting frequently. If at the end of the cooking time the vegetables have dried slightly, add a few tablespoons of water.
6. Serve as soon as you take the dish out of the oven.

Always try, wherever possible, to obtain the sort of bird from your butcher – poussin, pullet, cockerel or capon – to suit your particular recipe.

Poularde Demi-Deuil
Stuffed Chicken with Truffles

Serves 6. Preparation: 20 min Cooking: 1 hr 45 min

★ ★ ★

○ **1 1.8kg (3½ lb) pullet**
○ **salt and pepper**
○ **100g (4 oz) chicken breasts**
○ **100g (4 oz) chicken livers**
○ **100g (4 oz) ham**
○ **100g (4 oz) truffles (fresh or tinned)**
○ **100g (4 oz) barding fat**
○ **2 chicken stock cubes**
○ **2 litres (3½ pints) boiling water**

For the sauce:
○ **50g (2 oz) butter**
○ **50g (2 oz) flour**
○ **2 egg yolks**
○ **125g (5 oz) double cream**

1. Dissolve the chicken stock cubes in the boiling water. Rub the inside of the pullet with salt and pepper.
2. Chop the chicken breasts and ham. Dice the chicken livers. Slice the truffles.
3. Place some truffle slices underneath the breast skin of the bird as decoratively as you can.
4. Prepare the stuffing: place the chicken breasts, ham, chicken livers and half the remaining truffles in a bowl; season and mix well. Stuff the bird. Sew up the vent with a needle and thread. Bard the bird and secure with string.
5. Place the bird in a large saucepan and pour in the hot stock, covering it three-quarters of the way up. Cover the saucepan. Bring to the boil, then reduce the heat and simmer over a medium heat for 1 hour 30 minutes.
6. When cooked remove the bird from the stock and keep warm.
7. Reduce the stock to ½ litre (18 fl oz) by boiling briskly without a lid.
8. Melt the butter in another saucepan. Stir in the flour, using a wooden spoon. Then, before the flour has turned golden, slowly add the stock, passing it through a sieve. Bring back to the boil and leave the sauce to thicken for 5 minutes, stirring continuously. Remove the saucepan from the heat. Beat the eggs with the cream and add to the sauce, beating with a whisk for 1 minute. Add the remaining truffles.
9. Remove the bard and string from the bird. Place it on a serving dish and carve. Cut the stuffing into slices. Pour over a little sauce and serve the rest in a sauceboat.

Poulet aux Pommes de Terre
Sautéed Chicken with Potatoes

Serves 4. Preparation: 10 min Cooking: 1 hr 15 min

★ ★

○ **1 1.2kg (2¾ lb) chicken, jointed in 8 pieces**
○ **50g (2 oz) butter**
○ **30ml (2 tbls) oil**
○ **1 medium-sized onion**
○ **6 garlic cloves**
○ **6 fresh sage leaves**
○ **5ml (1 tsp) rosemary**
○ **250ml (9 fl oz) rosé wine**
○ **15ml (1 tbls) tomato concentrate**
○ **salt and pepper**
○ **4 large potatoes 150g (5 oz) each**
○ **15ml (1 tbls) chopped herbs or parsley**

1. Peel and wash the potatoes. Cut into 8 pieces downwards and put into a bowl filled with cold water.
2. Peel and slice the onions.
3. Heat the oil in a frying pan, add the butter and then the chicken pieces, onion, unpeeled garlic, sage and rosemary. Season.
4. Brown everything over a medium heat. Then add the tomato concentrate and mix well, turning the chicken pieces in the sauce (so that it absorbs the flavour). Then pour in the wine.
5. Drain the potatoes. Add to the rest and cover the pan. Cook over a very low heat for 1 hour. Turn the chicken pieces from time to time. If there is not enough liquid in the pan add 30ml (2 tbls) of water. At the end of the cooking time there should only be a small amount of liquid left.
6. Sprinkle with the chopped herbs or parsley. Serve at once.

Émincés de Poulet au Calvados

Serves 4. Preparation: 15 min Cooking: 30 min

Slices of Chicken with Calvados

★

- ○ **4 chicken breasts**
- ○ **500g (18 oz) button mushrooms**
- ○ **24 shallots, or pickling onions**
- ○ **50g (2 oz) butter**
- ○ **15ml (1 tbls) oil**
- ○ **45ml (3 tbls) calvados**
- ○ **200g (7 oz) cream**
- ○ **5ml (1 tsp) cornflour**
- ○ **30ml (2 tbls) cold water**
- ○ **salt and pepper**
- ○ **pinch nutmeg**

1. Cut each chicken breast into two, then slice lengthways. Peel the onions. Trim the mushrooms. Wash and drain the vegetables and wipe dry.
2. Heat the oil in a frying pan over a medium heat. Add the butter, then the slices of chicken. Brown all over, stirring frequently. Remove and put on one side.
3. Place the onions in the frying pan and gently sauté over a very low heat, stirring frequently.
4. Slice the mushrooms. Add to the onion and cook over a slightly higher heat.
5. When the mushrooms have begun to turn golden and their juices start to run, put the chicken back into the frying pan. Season with salt, pepper and grated nutmeg. Pour in the calvados.
6. Mix the cornflour with the cold water, and then blend in the cream. When the calvados has evaporated pour the cream into the frying pan and mix well. Cook for another 5 minutes, over a medium heat; the cream should take on a lovely golden colour. Serve at once.

Serve with allumettes or sauté potatoes.

Coq à la Bière

Serves 4. Preparation: 10 min Cooking: 1 hr 10 min

Cockerel in Beer

★ ★

- ○ **1 1.3kg (3 lb) oven-ready cockerel**
- ○ **6 shallots**
- ○ **80g (3 oz) butter**
- ○ **30ml (2 tbls) gin**
- ○ **1 bottle (½ pint) brown ale**
- ○ **200g (7 oz) cream**
- ○ **250g (9 oz) button mushrooms**
- ○ **30ml (2 tbls) chopped parsley**

1. Peel and finely chop the shallots.
2. Trim and wipe the mushrooms. Melt 50g (2 oz) of butter in a flameproof casserole over a low heat. Brown the cockerel all over for 15 minutes; remove from the casserole and put on one side.
3. Place the shallots in the casserole and sauté gently. Return the cockerel to the casserole; pour in the gin and set alight. Add a knob of butter and 45ml (3 tbls) cream. Stir well. Slice the mushrooms and add to the ingredients in the casserole.
4. Pour in the beer. Season and cover with a lid. Simmer for 40 minutes.
5. When the cockerel is cooked place on a serving dish. Cut into 4 large pieces and keep warm. Reduce the sauce to ¼ litre (9 fl oz, slightly less than ½ pint) over a high heat in the uncovered casserole. Then add the remaining cream and leave to reduce for a further 2 minutes.
6. Remove from the heat. Add the remaining knob of butter and pour over the cockerel. Sprinkle with parsley and serve at once.

Serve with allumettes.

Be careful when using nutmeg. You only need a pinch to flavour stuffings, sautéed dishes, cream sauces and omelettes. Buy it whole if possible, and grate it yourself as required. It retains its flavour better.

Poulet Chasseur

Serves 4. Preparation: 20 min Cooking: 1 hr

Chicken Chasseur

★ ★

○ 1 1.2kg (2¾ lb) chicken,
  jointed in 8 pieces
○ 50g (2 oz) butter
○ 15ml (1 tbls) oil
○ 15ml (1 tbls) flour
○ 400g (14 oz) button
  mushrooms
○ 500g (1 lb 2 oz) ripe tomatoes
○ 10 shallots
○ 1 sprig tarragon
○ 250ml (9 fl oz) dry white wine
○ salt and pepper

Bouquet garni:
○ 1 sprig thyme
○ 1 bay leaf
○ 3 sprigs parsley

1. Scald the tomatoes in boiling water for 30 seconds. Cool them under a running tap and peel them. Cut in half and squeeze to remove the seeds. Dice the pulp coarsely.
2. Peel and chop the shallots finely.
3. Strip the tarragon leaves. Tie together the herbs for the bouquet garni.
4. Trim, wipe and quarter the mushrooms.
5. Heat the oil in a flameproof casserole. Add the butter and brown the chicken joints all over. Remove from the casserole and leave to drain on a plate.
6. Add the shallots and mushrooms to the casserole. Gently fry, but do not let them colour too much. Then sprinkle on the flour; stir well, and pour in the wine and water.
7. Put the chicken joints back into the casserole. Add the tomatoes, tarragon leaves and the bouquet garni. Season and cover. Simmer for 40 minutes. Serve at once.

Accompany with boiled or steamed potatoes sprinkled with chopped tarragon.

Poule Bouillie aux Pâtes Fraîches

Serves 6. Preparation: 10 min
Cooking: 1 hr 45 min

Boiled Chicken with Fresh Noodles

★ ★

○ 1 1.5kg (3¼ lb) young boiling
  fowl, trussed
○ 3 carrots
○ 2 celery stalks
○ 50g (2 oz) button mushrooms
○ 1 onion
○ 2 cloves
○ 6 peppercorns
○ 2 chicken stock cubes
○ 300g (11 oz) fresh noodles
○ 50g (2 oz) butter
○ grated Gruyère cheese
○ salt and pepper
○ 250ml (9 fl oz) hot water

Bouquet garni:
○ 1 sprig thyme
○ 1 bay leaf
○ 4 sprigs parsley

1. Prepare and wash the vegetables. Spike the onion with the cloves. Place the bird in a large saucepan. Add the vegetables, bouquet garni and peppercorns. Season sparingly with salt (the stock cube will already have been salted).
2. Dissolve the stock cubes in 250ml (9 fl oz) hot water. Pour the stock into the saucepan; add enough cold water to cover the bird. Put a lid on the pan and simmer over a low heat for 1 hour 30 minutes.
3. When the bird is cooked, remove from the stock, carve and arrange the pieces in a deep dish. Pour a ladleful of stock over and keep warm.
4. Remove the vegetables from the stock and dice them. Discard the bouquet garni.
5. Cook the noodles in the stock: they should be *al dente* – slightly firm (not soft). Drain and add the vegetables and butter. Mix together well and place on top of the chicken joints. Sprinkle with the grated Gruyère and serve at once.

Rice and peas may be cooked in the stock instead of fresh pasta.

Poulet aux Écrevisses

Serves 6. Preparation and cooking: 1 hr 15 min

Chicken with Crayfish

★ ★ ★

○ 1 1.6kg (3½ lb) chicken,
   jointed in 8 pieces
○ 30g (1¼ oz) butter
○ 1 unpeeled garlic clove crushed
○ 100g (4 oz) fresh tomato pulp
○ 30ml (2 tbls) cognac
○ 100ml (3½ fl oz) dry white
   wine
○ 125g (5 oz) cream
○ salt and pepper
○ 15ml (1 tbls) chopped parsley
   and tarragon

For the crayfish:
○ 24 crayfish, washed and gutted
○ 1 finely chopped onion
○ 2 finely chopped shallots
○ 1 sliced carrot
○ 40g (1¾ oz) butter
○ 1 pinch thyme
○ ½ bay leaf
○ 30ml (2 tbls) cognac
○ 250ml (9 fl oz) dry white wine
○ salt and pepper

1. Melt the butter in a flameproof casserole and gently fry the
   chicken joints over a very low heat until lightly browned. Season,
   pour in the cognac, wine, garlic and tomato pulp. Cover with a
   lid and simmer for 40 minutes, over a low heat.
2. Meanwhile, prepare the crayfish in the 'Bordeaux' manner: melt
   the butter in a pan and sauté the onion, carrot and shallots until
   lightly browned. Then add the crayfish, salt, pepper, thyme and
   bay leaf. Sauté the crayfish over a high heat until they turn red.
   Then pour in the cognac and wine. Cover the pan and cook for
   10 minutes.
3. At the end of that time, shell 18 crayfish. Put the remaining 6
   aside for garnishing. Reserve the cooking juices.
4. When the chicken is cooked, put on one side with the crayfish.
   Add the cooking juices from the crayfish to the stock in the
   casserole. Reduce uncovered over a high heat until 200ml (7 fl oz)
   of liquid remains. Stir in the cream and put the chicken joints
   and crayfish back into the casserole. Simmer for 5 minutes.
   Check the seasoning.
5. Place the chicken joints and crayfish on a serving dish. Garnish
   with the 6 remaining crayfish. Pour over the sauce, passing it
   through a sieve. Sprinkle with herbs and serve at once.

Chicken with crayfish is one of the great classic dishes of French
cuisine. Before cooking the crayfish you must be sure to clean them
thoroughly. To do this, tug very strongly on the central ribs of the
tail, and the guts will come out cleanly.

Petit Sauté de Poulet aux Girolles

Serves 4. Preparation: 15 min
Cooking: 30 min

Sautéed Chicken Breasts with Mushrooms

★

○ 4 chicken breasts
○ 50g (2 oz) butter
○ juice of ½ lemon
○ 500g (1 lb 2 oz) chanterelle
   mushrooms
○ 200g (7 oz) cream
○ 15ml (1 tbls) chopped herbs:
   parsley, chervil, tarragon,
   chives
○ salt and pepper

1. Clean the mushrooms.
2. Cook the mushrooms in a frying pan over a medium heat, stirring
   from time to time so that the juices run.
3. When all the juices have run add a knob of butter to the
   mushrooms and simmer for 15 minutes.
4. Meanwhile, prepare the chicken breasts. Slice them in two and
   flatten each side with the blade of a knife.
5. Melt the rest of the butter in a heavy pan over a low heat and
   brown the chicken breasts on both sides. Add the lemon juice
   and season to taste. Cover and simmer for 10 minutes.
6. Then add the mushrooms to the chicken in the pan. Pour in the
   cream, stir well and simmer, uncovered, for 5 minutes. The cream
   should turn a slightly golden colour.
7. Serve very hot sprinkled with herbs.

You can replace the chanterelles with other kinds of mushrooms for
this recipe.

*If you strip the stem from a sprig of garden thyme and roll the leaves and dried up flowers between your
fingers, you will obtain a small quantity of what in France is known as* fleurs de thym. *It has a stronger
flavour than the dried thyme you can buy in most shops.*

Coquelets à la Bière

Poussins in Beer

Serves 6. Preparation: 15 min Cooking: 1 hr

★

- ○ **3 poussins**
- ○ **1 medium-sized onion**
- ○ **30ml (2 tbls) gin**
- ○ **300g (11 oz) button mushrooms**
- ○ **50g (2 oz) butter**
- ○ **125g (4 oz) cream**
- ○ **1 bottle (½ pint) brown ale**
- ○ **24 juniper berries**
- ○ **salt and pepper**
- ○ **1 small bunch parsley**

1. Rub the inside of the poussins with salt and pepper
2. Peel and finely chop the onion. Trim and wipe the mushrooms. Chop the parsley coarsely.
3. Melt the butter in a heavy pan over a low heat. Brown the poussins on all sides for about 15 minutes. Remove from the heat. Place the onion in the pan and fry gently.
4. Slice the mushrooms thinly. When the onion has begun to turn golden add the mushrooms and fry until the juices run.
5. Place the poussins back in the pan. Season. Moisten with gin and set alight. Pour in the beer and add the juniper berries. Simmer over a medium heat for 25 minutes, turning the poussins frequently. At the end of the cooking time the sauce should be of a thick consistency.
6. When the poussins are cooked remove from the pan and put on a serving dish. With a sharp knife, cut the breasts into two, from the neck to the tail. Place the mushrooms inside the poussins.
7. Blend the cream with the sauce in the pan. Bring to the boil and cook for 1 minute beating with a whisk. Pour over the poussins. Sprinkle with chopped parsley and serve at once.

Poulet en Papillotes

Chicken Quarters in Foil

Serves 4. Preparation: 20 min Cooking: 1 hr

★

- ○ **1 1.2kg (2¾ lb) chicken, cut into quarters**
- ○ **45ml (3 tbls) olive oil**
- ○ **1 medium-sized onion**
- ○ **2 garlic cloves**
- ○ **500g (1 lb 2 oz) ripe tomatoes**
- ○ **24 small black olives**
- ○ **5ml (1 tsp) oregano**
- ○ **2 bay leaves**
- ○ **salt and pepper**
- ○ **coarse salt**

1. Scald the tomatoes in boiling water for 30 seconds. Cool under running water and peel. Cut in half, squeeze to remove seeds, and dice. Mash with a fork.
2. Peel the garlic cloves. Crush, or chop them very finely. Add to the tomato purée.
3. Peel and finely chop the onion. Add to the tomato purée together with the oregano, salt, olives and 30ml (2 tbls) of olive oil. Mix well.
4. Cut four pieces off a large sheet of greaseproof paper or foil. Brush with olive oil. Place a chicken quarter in the centre of each; cover with the sauce and garnish with a half bay leaf. Fold over the foil to enclose the chicken quarter completely.
5. Preheat the oven to 220°C (425°F; gas mark 7). Cover the bottom of a baking tray with coarse salt 1cm (½ inch) thick; place the chicken *en papillotes* on top. The salt will prevent the meat from burning whilst cooking at a very high temperature on a hot baking sheet.
6. Cook for 45 minutes; open the foil, remove the bay leaves and cook for another 15 minutes.

Serve with a green salad.

Coq au Vin
Cockerel in Wine

Serves 6. Preparation: 15 min Cooking: 1 hr 45 min

★ ★

- ○ 1 2.5kg (5½ lb) cockerel, jointed in 12 pieces
- ○ 1 bottle red wine
- ○ 30ml (2 tbls) oil
- ○ 60g (2½ oz) butter
- ○ 15ml (1 tbls) flour
- ○ 100g (4 oz) smoked streaky bacon
- ○ 24 shallots, or pickling onions
- ○ 24 button mushrooms
- ○ 2 unpeeled garlic cloves
- ○ 1 sugar lump
- ○ salt and pepper
- ○ pinch nutmeg
- ○ 15ml (1 tbls) cognac
- ○ 30ml (2 tbls) chopped herbs: parsley, chervil, chives, tarragon

Bouquet garni:
- ○ 1 sprig thyme
- ○ 1 bay leaf
- ○ 1 sprig rosemary

For the croûtons:
- ○ 12 slices of French bread
- ○ 100g (4 oz) butter

Optional:
- ○ a few truffle slices, or extra mushrooms

1. Peel the onion. Cut the bacon into strips.
2. Heat the oil in a flameproof casserole over a medium heat. Add the butter and fry the chicken joints until lightly browned. Remove and put on one side.
3. Pour away half of the cooking fat. Add the onions and bacon and fry gently. Then sprinkle in the flour, stirring well, and pour in the wine.
4. When the sauce starts to boil, add the bouquet garni, unpeeled garlic, sugar, and the chicken joints. Season with salt, pepper and grated nutmeg. Cover with a lid and simmer over a very low heat for 1 hour 15 minutes.
5. At the end of 15 minutes, trim and wipe the mushrooms. Add to the casserole.
6. After 1 hour 15 minutes check whether the joints are tender and the meat falls away easily from the bones. If cooked, remove at once and keep warm in a serving dish.
7. Pour the cognac into the casserole. Reduce the sauce to about ⅓ litre (about ½ pint) by boiling uncovered for 5 minutes.
8. Meanwhile, prepare the croûtons. Cut the crusts off the bread and cut into squares. Heat the butter in a frying pan and fry the bread briskly.
9. Add the truffles to the sauce and pour over the chicken joints. Arrange the croûtons round. Sprinkle with chopped herbs and serve at once.

Poulet au Riesling
Chicken in Riesling

Serves 6. Preparation: 10 min Cooking: 1 hr 20 min

★ ★

- ○ 1 1.8kg (4 lb) chicken, jointed in 12 pieces
- ○ 50g (2 oz) butter
- ○ 30ml (2 tbls) oil
- ○ 20 shallots
- ○ 100ml (3½ fl oz) cognac
- ○ 1 half-bottle Riesling
- ○ 125g (4 oz) cream
- ○ salt and pepper

1. Peel and chop the shallots finely.
2. In a flameproof casserole heat the oil, add the butter and chicken joints. Brown all over. Season.
3. When the chicken joints have browned, remove from casserole and put on one side. Pour away half the cooking fat and gently fry the shallots. Return the chicken joints and pour in the cognac.
4. Stir everything together well until the cognac has evaporated. Then moisten with wine and simmer uncovered for about 45 minutes.
5. At the end of the cooking time, remove the chicken joints and place on a serving dish. Keep warm.
6. Reduce the sauce to 150ml (5 fl oz; ¼ pint approx). Then stir in the cream and reduce for 2 minutes more.
7. Check the seasoning and pour the sauce over the chicken joints.

Serve with boiled or steamed potatoes, sprinkled with parsley.

Poulet Sauce Poulette

Serves 4. Preparation: 10 min Cooking: 1 hr 15 min

Chicken Sauce Poulette

★★

○ 1 1.2kg (2¾ lb) chicken, trussed
○ 2 medium-sized carrots
○ 1 celery stalk
○ 1 leek
○ 80g (3 oz) butter
○ 2 shallots, or pickling onions
○ 15ml (1 tbls) flour
○ 1 egg yolk
○ 30ml (2 tbls) cream
○ 15ml (1 tbls) chopped parsley
○ juice of 1 lemon

1. Prepare and wash the vegetables.
2. Place the chicken with the vegetables in a large saucepan. Cover with just enough cold water: you need about 2 litres (88 fl oz; 3½ pints). Cook over a medium heat.
3. When the water starts to boil, skim. Season with salt. Turn the heat down and simmer for about 1 hour.
4. 10 minutes before the end of the cooking time prepare the sauce. Peel and finely chop the onions. Melt the butter in a saucepan and gently sauté the onions, but do not let them brown. Remove from heat.
5. Remove the chicken from the stock. Place on a serving dish, carve, and keep warm.
6. Reserve ½ litre (18 fl oz; just under 1 pint) of the chicken stock. Put the rest back over a medium heat. Add the flour gradually and stir well; then slowly pour in the reserved stock, stirring continuously. Boil the sauce for 5 minutes, then remove from heat.
7. Beat the egg yolk and the cream together. Pour this mixture into the sauce, beating with a whisk for 1 minute. Add the juice of one lemon, together with the chopped parsley. Check the seasoning.
8. Pour some of the sauce over the chicken and serve the rest in a sauceboat.

Serve with boiled rice that has been allowed to dry slightly in the oven.

Blancs de Poulet Surprise

Serves 4. Preparation: 10 min Cooking: 20 min

Surprise Chicken Breasts

★★

○ 4 chicken breasts
○ 4 thin slices ham
○ 8 thin slices Emmenthal or Gouda cheese
○ 8 fresh basil leaves
○ 80g (3 oz) butter
○ 100ml (3½ fl oz) port, dry marsala, or sherry
○ salt and pepper

1. Cut each chicken breast into two. Flatten each slice with the blade of a knife. Cut each slice of ham into two lengthways.
2. Place a slice of ham on each chicken breast then cover with a slice of cheese, and garnish with one basil leaf.
3. Fold each slice over, and secure the edge with 2 cocktail sticks.
4. Melt the butter in a heavy pan over a low heat. Gently fry the chicken pieces for 3 minutes on each side. Season, and moisten with wine. Cover the pan and simmer for 15 minutes over a very low heat. Turn the chicken pieces occasionally while cooking.
5. Place the chicken pieces on a serving dish. If necessary, deglaze the pan by adding 30ml (2 tbls) of water to the sauce. Pour the sauce over the chicken.

Serve with buttered peas or fresh spinach.

How to prepare fried chicken successfully. Cut into pieces of equal size. Dip them in batter or cover with breadcrumbs. To do this, coat each piece with flour. Then dip in beaten egg and roll in the breadcrumbs, pressing down well to ensure they adhere firmly to the meat.

Coquelets aux Herbes

Serves 6. Preparation: 5 min Cooking: 50 min

Poussins with Herbs

★

- 3 poussins
- 200g (7 oz) smoked streaky bacon
- 30ml (2 tbls) oil
- 50g (2 oz) butter
- 2 bay leaves
- 2 sprigs thyme
- 10 sprigs parsley
- 20 sprigs chervil
- 2 sprigs tarragon
- 1 small bunch chives
- salt and pepper
- 30ml (2 tbls) water

1. Rub the inside of the poussins with salt and pepper.
2. Cut the bacon into strips. Chop the herbs coarsely, having removed the stalks.
3. Heat the oil in a heavy pan and gently fry the bacon over a low heat for 10 minutes. Remove with a slotted spoon and put on one side.
4. Add half the butter to the fat in the pan. Brown the poussins on all sides over a low heat for about 15 minutes. Add the thyme and bay leaves. Season with salt and pepper. Cover with a lid and cook for another 15 minutes, stirring frequently.
5. When the poussins are cooked, put the bacon strips back into the pan. Add the chopped herbs, water and remaining butter. Continue cooking over a low heat for 5 minutes, turning the poussins in the sauce. Serve at once.

Serve with small sautéed potatoes.

Chapon à la Sauce aux Noix

Serves 8. Preparation and cooking: 2 hr 10 min

Roast Capon with Walnut Sauce

★★★

- 1 2kg (4½ lb) capon
- salt and pepper
- 30ml (2 tbls) oil

For the sauce:
- 4 finely chopped shallots
- 50g (2 oz) butter
- 15ml (1 tbls) flour
- 1 chicken stock cube
- 30ml (2 tbls) wine vinegar
- 1 crushed clove
- pinch cinnamon
- pinch cayenne pepper
- ½ bay leaf
- 100g (4 oz) chopped walnuts
- juice of ½ orange
- pinch saffron
- salt and pepper
- 15ml (1 tbls) chopped parsley

For the garnish:
- 16 green walnuts
- ½ orange

1. Preheat the oven to 220°C (425°F; gas mark 7). Rub the inside of the capon with salt and pepper. Brush the outside with oil. Grease an ovenproof dish and place the capon in it.
2. Cook in the oven for 30 minutes, then turn the heat down to 200°C (400°F; gas mark 6) and cook for another 30 minutes, adding a little water to the dish whenever the cooking juices start to brown. Baste the capon with these juices frequently.
3. After 1 hour of cooking, reduce the heat further to 190°C (375°F; gas mark 5) and continue cooking for another hour, basting frequently.
4. 15 minutes before the end of the time, prepare the sauce. Dissolve the chicken stock cube in ½ litre (18 fl oz; just under 1 pint) of boiling water. Melt the butter in a saucepan and gently fry the shallots until lightly brown. Then sprinkle on the flour and pour in the hot stock, stirring all the time to prevent the sauce becoming lumpy. Add the vinegar, clove, cinnamon, cayenne pepper, bay leaf, parsley, and pinch of saffron for colouring. Season sparingly with salt (the stock will already have been salted) and add some pepper. Simmer for 10 minutes, stirring all the time; then add the juice from half an orange and the walnuts. Mix together well for another minute. Pour the sauce into a sauceboat.
5. Peel and slice the other half of the orange, then cut into small segments.
6. Arrange the capon on a serving dish, garnished with the green walnuts and orange segments.
7. Pour 100ml (3½ fl oz) of water into the dish the capon was cooked in. Deglaze the sauce and pour it into another sauceboat.
8. Serve the capon with the two sauces.

A few suggestions to accompany this dish: sautéed mushrooms, buttered green vegetables, braised chicory or celery hearts.

Poulet au Vinaigre

Serves 4. Preparation: 15 min Cooking: 55 min

Chicken in Tarragon Wine Vinegar

★★

- ○ 1 1.2kg (2¾ lb) chicken, jointed in 8 pieces
- ○ 150g (6 oz) butter
- ○ salt and pepper
- ○ 100ml (3½ fl oz) dry white wine
- ○ 100ml (3½ fl oz) tarragon wine vinegar
- ○ 1 tin 400g (14 oz) peeled tomatoes
- ○ 250g (9 oz) button mushrooms
- ○ 1 small bunch parsley

For the croûtons:
- ○ 8 slices of French bread
- ○ 50g (2 oz) butter

1. Cut the tinned tomatoes in half and remove the seeds. Mash with a fork and put in a bowl with their juice.
2. In a heavy pan, melt 50g (2 oz) of butter and brown the chicken joints on all sides. Season. Add the vinegar and turn the chicken frequently in the sauce (to moisten the meat well).
3. When the vinegar has completely evaporated, add the wine, reduce by half, then add the tomatoes and cover the pan. Simmer for 30 minutes over a low heat, turning the chicken joints occasionally.
4. Meanwhile, trim and wipe the mushrooms, and slice them thinly. Melt a knob of butter in a frying pan and sauté the mushrooms. When all their juices have run out and they have turned golden, remove from the heat and keep warm.
5. 5 minutes before the end of the cooking time, prepare the croûtons. Melt the butter in a frying pan and briskly fry the slices of bread. Drain on kitchen paper.
6. When the chicken is cooked, remove from the pan and place on a serving dish. Arrange the mushrooms on top and keep warm.
7. Cut the remaining 100g (4 oz) of butter into knobs, and add one by one to the cooking pan, folding them into the sauce a little at a time, using a whisk. Pour the sauce, which should be creamy and frothy, over the chicken joints.
8. Garnish with the croûtons and small sprigs of parsley. Serve at once.

Poulet en Escabèche

Serves 4. Preparation: 5 min Cooking: 20 min To be served cold

Cold Chicken Breasts in Vinegar Sauce

★

- ○ 4 chicken breasts
- ○ 90ml (6 tbls) oil
- ○ 4 garlic cloves
- ○ 1 medium-sized onion
- ○ 5ml (1 tsp) rosemary
- ○ 1 small dried chilli
- ○ 200ml (7 fl oz) white wine vinegar
- ○ salt

1. Peel and slice the onion finely. Peel the garlic. Divide each chicken breast into two. Flatten each slice with the blade of a knife.
2. Heat the oil in a frying pan over a medium heat. Fry each chicken breast for 4 to 6 minutes on each side. Season with salt. When cooked, place in a deep ovenproof dish.
3. Add the garlic cloves, sliced onion, rosemary, and flaked chilli to the frying pan. When the garlic and onion are golden, pour in the vinegar and boil for 5 minutes. Add a little more salt, then pour the boiling sauce over the chicken pieces.

This dish is eaten cold. Leave it to stand one or two days in the refrigerator, turning the chicken pieces once or twice so that the sauce penetrates the meat.

To make sure that chicken joints are well cooked, add them to the casserole or sauté pan 10 minutes before the breast and wings.

Cuisses de Poulet aux Épinards

Serves 4. Preparation and cooking: 1 hr 10 min

Chicken Legs with Spinach

★★

- ○ **4 chicken legs**
- ○ **100g (4 oz) butter**
- ○ **30ml (2 tbls) oil**
- ○ **1 medium-sized onion**
- ○ **100ml (3½ fl oz) dry white wine**
- ○ **200ml (7 fl oz) warm water**
- ○ **500g (1 lb 2 oz) spinach**
- ○ **125g (4 oz) cream**
- ○ **5ml (1 tsp) cornflour**
- ○ **30ml (2 tbls) cold water**
- ○ **1 egg yolk**
- ○ **50g (2 oz) grated Parmesan cheese**
- ○ **salt and pepper**

1. Peel and chop the onion finely.
2. Heat the oil in a heavy pan. Add 50g (2 oz) of butter and brown the chicken legs all over. Remove from the pan and put on one side.
3. Pour away half the cooking fat, sauté the onion and put the chicken legs back into the pan. Season. Add the wine and warm water. Cover and simmer for 50 minutes over a low heat, turning the chicken from time to time.
4. 25 minutes before the end of the time, clean, wash and blanch the spinach in a large quantity of boiling salted water for 5 minutes, and strain.
5. Melt the remaining butter in a frying pan over a low heat. Add the spinach and sauté for 5 minutes. Turn off the heat, sprinkle with the grated cheese, mix in well, and cover with a lid to keep warm.
6. In a bowl, beat the egg yolk with the cream, using a fork. Mix the cornflour with cold water and blend with the egg/cream mixture.
7. When the chicken legs are cooked, remove from the pan and arrange on a serving dish. Keep warm.
8. Pour the contents of the bowl into the pan. Mix with the cooking juices, using a whisk, and boil for 1 minute beating all the time. Remove from heat.
9. Place the spinach around the chicken and pour the sauce over. Serve at once.

Poulet Gratiné

Serves 4. Preparation and cooking: 1 hr 15 min

Chicken Gratin

★★

- ○ **1 1.2kg (2¾ lb) chicken, jointed in 8 pieces**
- ○ **50g (2 oz) butter**
- ○ **15ml (1 tbls) oil**
- ○ **salt**

For the sauce:
- ○ **50g (2 oz) butter**
- ○ **50g (2 oz) flour**
- ○ **½ litre (18 fl oz) warm milk**
- ○ **125g (4 oz) cream**
- ○ **100g (4 oz) grated Emmenthal cheese**
- ○ **salt and pepper**
- ○ **pinch nutmeg**

1. In a heavy pan, heat the oil. Add 50g (2 oz) of butter and brown the chicken joints all over. Then add 100ml (3½ fl oz) of water. Season with salt.
2. Cover the pan and simmer for 45 minutes over a low heat, turning the chicken joints occasionally.
3. 15 minutes before the end of cooking time, prepare the sauce. Melt the butter in a saucepan, sprinkle in the flour, and work in. Then add the warm milk a drop at a time, stirring continuously. Season with salt, pepper and grated nutmeg. Add the cream and grated cheese. Remove from the heat and mix everything together well.
4. Preheat the oven to 220°C (425°F; gas mark 7). When the chicken is cooked, remove from the pan and arrange in an ovenproof dish. Pour over the cheese sauce and cook in the oven for 15 minutes, until it browns.
5. Serve in the dish.

Accompany with braised vegetables such as celery or chicory.

Dindonneau Farci en Cocotte

Serves 8. Preparation: 15 min Cooking: 15 min

Braised Stuffed Turkey

★★★

○ **1 young 2.2kg (5 lb) turkey**
○ **200g (7 oz) cooked ham**
○ **200g (7 oz) pork sausagemeat**
○ **200g (7 oz) bread, crusts removed**
○ **200ml (7 fl oz) warm milk**
○ **2 small truffles or mushrooms**
○ **1 chicken stock cube**
○ **½ litre (1 pint) warm water**
○ **salt and pepper**
○ **nutmeg**
○ **100ml (3½ fl oz) groundnut oil**
○ **125g (4½ oz) butter**
○ **6 fresh sage leaves**
○ **1 small sprig rosemary**

1. Soak the bread in warm milk. Chop the ham.
2. Mash the bread in a bowl, using a fork. Add the sausagemeat and chopped ham. Mix all ingredients well. Cut one truffle into thin strips and add to the bowl. Season with salt, pepper and grated nutmeg and mix again.
3. Fill the turkey with the stuffing, and sew the vent with a needle and thread.
4. Dissolve the chicken stock in warm water.
5. Heat the oil in a large flameproof casserole. Add 50g (2 oz) of butter, the sage and rosemary. Brown the turkey on all sides over a medium heat, making sure the butter does not burn. Season with salt and pepper.
6. Pour half the stock into the casserole and cover tightly with a lid. Cook over a low heat for 2 hours, adding the remaining stock if necessary during the cooking. When the turkey is cooked, there should be hardly any cooking juices remaining – about 200ml (7 fl oz).
7. Remove the turkey from the casserole and place on a serving dish. Using a spoon, skim as much fat as possible from the cooking juices and reduce over a brisk heat if necessary, then turn the heat down.
8. Add the remaining butter to the casserole, beating it into the juices with a whisk. The sauce should be smooth and creamy. Cut the remaining truffle into thin strips, add to the sauce and pour over the turkey. Serve at once.

Serve with braised celery hearts, chicory or a smooth purée of celeriac.

Filets de Dinde au Marsala

Serves 4. Preparation: 5 min Cooking: 55 min

Turkey Breasts in Marsala

★★

○ **8 turkey breasts, about 100g (4 oz) each**
○ **80g (3 oz) butter**
○ **100ml (3½ fl oz) dry Marsala**
○ **100ml (3½ fl oz) milk**
○ **250g (9 oz) ripe tomatoes**
○ **30ml (2 tbls) cream**
○ **salt and pepper**
○ **nutmeg**

1. Wash the tomatoes and quarter them. Pass them through the fine mesh of a vegetable mill.
2. Melt the butter in a large frying pan and lightly brown the turkey breasts on both sides. Season with salt, pepper and grated nutmeg.
3. Add the Marsala, milk and tomato purée. Cover the frying pan loosely.
4. Simmer over a low heat for 35 minutes, turning the turkey in the sauce two or three times.
5. Remove the turkey breasts from the frying pan and place on a serving dish. Pour the cream into the pan, boil the sauce for 1 or 2 minutes until it thickens, then pour over the turkey. Serve at once.

Serve with french beans, sprinkled with parsley, or small sauté potatoes.

A sautéed fowl should always be cooked in a pan or casserole, uncovered; otherwise it is braised.

Dinde au Chocolat

Serves 8-10. Preparation and cooking: 2 hr

Turkey with Chocolate Sauce

★★★

○ 1 2.5kg (5½ lb) turkey, jointed (10 pieces)
○ 60ml (4 tbls) goose fat or dripping
○ salt

For the sauce:
○ ¾ litre (slightly over 1¼ pint) chicken stock, preferably home-made
○ 1 small chilli, flaked
○ 100g (4 oz) blanched almonds
○ 1 clove garlic, peeled
○ 1 medium-sized onion, finely chopped
○ 2ml (½ tsp) powdered cinnamon
○ 1 clove, crushed
○ 2ml (½ tsp) powdered coriander seeds
○ 30ml (2 tbls) sultanas
○ 2ml (½ tsp) aniseed
○ 15ml (1 tbls) sesame seeds
○ 60ml (4 tbls) unsweetened cocoa or 50g (2 oz) bitter chocolate
○ salt and pepper

1. Place the turkey pieces in a flameproof casserole, cover with cold water and bring to the boil. Season with salt and cook over a low heat for 1 hour 15 minutes.
2. Meanwhile, prepare the sauce. Put all the ingredients (except the chocolate or cocoa) in the bowl of an electric mixer and add half the stock. Blend at top speed until you obtain a purée.
3. Melt 15ml (1 tbls) of goose fat or dripping in a saucepan. Add the sauce, the remaining stock and the chocolate. Season with salt and pepper. Bring to the boil and simmer for 5 minutes, stirring all the time, then turn the heat off.
4. Remove the turkey pieces from the casserole, drain and wipe with kitchen paper.
5. Melt the remaining goose fat or dripping in the casserole and brown the turkey pieces on each side. Then simmer, uncovered, for 30 minutes, adding the sauce a little at a time, every 10 minutes.
6. When the turkey is cooked, place on a serving dish and cover with the sauce.

Serve this turkey the Mexican way: sprinkled with toasted sesame seeds and accompanied by *tortillas*. *Tortillas* are pancakes made with a thick batter, rich in eggs. They are cooked in butter in a frying pan or a crêpe pan. As soon as you pour the batter into the frying pan, sprinkle with freshly cooked corn grains, then fold the pancake over. *Tortillas* are served with fresh cream and sprinkled with chopped parsley.

Dinde Farcie aux Trois Fruits

Serves 8. Preparation: 20 min Cooking: 2 hr 15 min

Roast Turkey with Three Fruit Stuffing

★★

○ 1 young 2.5kg (5½ lb) turkey
○ 150g (5 oz) prunes
○ 12 chestnuts
○ 2 cooking apples
○ 200g (7 oz) pork sausagemeat
○ 200g (7 oz) ham
○ 30ml (2 tbls) Armagnac
○ the turkey liver
○ 1 egg
○ salt and pepper
○ nutmeg
○ 30ml (2 tbls) oil

1. Soak the prunes in lukewarm water for 1 hour, then stone them.
2. Chop the ham and dice the turkey liver. Flake the chestnuts. Peel and coarsely grate the apples.
3. Put all these ingredients into a bowl and add the sausagemeat and egg. Season with salt, pepper and grated nutmeg. Mix well, sprinkle over with Armagnac, and mix once more.
4. Preheat the oven to 200°C (400°F; gas mark 6). Rub the inside of the turkey with salt and pepper. Fill the turkey with the stuffing and sew the vent with a needle and thread. Brush with oil and place in an ovenproof dish.
5. Roast for 30 minutes at 200°C (400°F; gas mark 6), then for 1 hour at 190°C (375°F; gas mark 5), then reduce the heat to 180°C (350°F; gas mark 4) and cook for a further 45 minutes. Baste frequently with the cooking juices, adding a few tablespoons of water whenever the juices start to caramelize.
6. When the turkey is ready, place it on a serving dish. Deglaze the cooking juices with a little water and pour into a sauceboat. Serve at once.

Serve with corn salad (known also as lamb's lettuce) seasoned with olive oil and vinegar.

Estouffat de Dinde aux Oignons

Casserole of Turkey with Onions

Serves 4. Preparation and cooking: 1 hr 35 min

★

○ **900g (2 lb) legs and breasts of turkey**
○ **1kg (2¼ lb) onions**
○ **60g (2½ oz) butter**
○ **250ml (9 fl oz) beer**
○ **salt and pepper**

1. Peel and finely slice the onions. Put into a sauté pan (without any cooking fat), cover the pan and sauté for 20 minutes over a low heat, stirring from time to time.
2. Meanwhile, cut the turkey joints into square chunks, about 3 cm (1 inch) thick, and remove the bones.
3. Melt the butter in a frying pan and brown the turkey pieces on all sides. Season with salt and pepper.
4. When the onions have cooked for approximately 20 minutes, add the turkey pieces and mix well.
5. Pour over the beer, cover the sauté pan and cook for 1 hour over a low heat, until there is no liquid left in the pan.
6. Serve very hot.

Serve with *gnocchi au gratin* or polenta. *Gnocchi* are a kind of dumplings made of *pâté à choux* into which a purée is beaten. Polenta is corn meal, made from maize, which is dried and ground.

Saucisson de Dinde

Turkey Sausage

Serves 6. Preparation: 25 min Cooking: 1 hr 15 min
To be served cold
★ ★ ★

○ **1kg (2½ lb) turkey legs and breasts**
○ **200g (7 oz) ham**
○ **100g (4 oz) stale bread, without crusts**
○ **100ml (3½ fl oz) warm milk**
○ **100g (4 oz) grated Gruyère**
○ **2 eggs**
○ **salt and pepper**
○ **nutmeg**
○ **2 chicken stock cubes**
○ **1 onion**
○ **1 carrot**
○ **1 stalk celery**
○ **1 clove**

1. Remove the bones from the turkey legs, and discard the skin from the legs and breasts. Coarsely chop the meat. Finely chop the ham. Soak the bread in warm milk then mash it with a fork.
2. Put the turkey, ham, bread and Gruyère in a bowl. Season with salt, pepper and grated nutmeg. Add the eggs and mix all ingredients well, using a fork. Roll this mixture into a large sausage shape.
3. Wash and peel the vegetables. Spike the onion with the clove. Bring 2 litres (3½ pints) of water to the boil in a large saucepan. Add the vegetables and chicken stock cubes.
4. Lay the turkey sausage on a clean cloth and roll up tightly. Secure the ends with string. Plunge into the saucepan and cook for 1 hour 15 minutes over a low heat.
5. Remove the sausage from the saucepan and leave to cool, then remove string and cloth. Cut into thick slices.

Serve with mayonnaise: mayonnaise with lemon, or with herbs, and accompany with raw vegetables and salad.

A top quality fowl should have a smooth white skin, its flesh should be firm and its legs plump.

The flesh of a well cooked fowl should be neither bloody nor dry. To check whether the fowl is cooked or not, insert a needle into the flesh of the thigh – the juice which spurts out should be transparent. If it is slightly pink, continue cooking. If there is not much liquid left in the cooking dish, add a little water or white wine (this only applies to oven roast fowls). Mix the cooking juices into the liquid, boil for 1 minute, then add a knob of butter.

Rôti de Dinde au Céleri

Serves 4. Preparation: 10 min Cooking: 1 hr 10 min

Roast Turkey with Celery

★

○ **800g (1¾ lb) turkey breasts**
○ **2 celery hearts**
○ **4 slices smoked lean bacon**
○ **4 cloves garlic**
○ **2.5ml (½ tsp) powdered cinnamon**
○ **15ml (1 tbls) oil**
○ **salt and pepper**
○ **60ml (4 tbls) cognac**

1. Preheat the oven to 190°C (375°F; gas mark 5).
2. Clean and wash the celery hearts, and cut into thin slices.
3. Grease an ovenproof dish. Put the celery slices and unpeeled garlic cloves into the dish.
4. Roll the turkey breasts together and secure with a piece of string to look like a roast. Place on top of the celery hearts. Lay the bacon slices on top of the turkey.
5. Sprinkle with cinnamon, salt and pepper and cook in the oven for 1 hour 10 minutes, basting frequently with the cooking juices or, if necessary, with a little water.
6. When the turkey roast is cooked, remove from the oven. Sprinkle with cognac, set alight and bring to the table.

Dindonneau aux Airelles

Serves 6. Preparation and cooking: 2 hr 15 min

Roast Turkey with Bilberry (or Cranberry) Sauce

★★

○ **1 young 2kg (4½ lb) turkey**
○ **100g (4 oz) barding fat, or streaky bacon**
○ **1 carrot**
○ **1 onion**
○ **1 celery stalk**
○ **1 sprig thyme**
○ **1 chicken stock cube**
○ **½ litre (1 pint) warm water**
○ **200ml (7 fl oz) dry white wine**
○ **250g (9 oz) cream**
○ **small punnet of bilberries or cranberries (fresh if possible)**
○ **salt and pepper**

1. Rub the inside of the turkey with salt and pepper. Place the barding fat on the breast and secure with string. Place the turkey in an ovenproof dish.
2. Peel, wash and finely slice the vegetables. Place around the turkey, with the thyme.
3. Preheat the oven to 200°C (400°F; gas mark 6). Dissolve the chicken stock cube in warm water and pour one third into the dish.
4. Cook in the oven for 45 minutes, adding more stock as required. Then reduce the heat to 190°C (375°F; gas mark 5) and cook for another 30 minutes.
5. When the cooking time is over, remove the barding fat and continue cooking for another ½ hour, turning the heat down to 180°C (350°F; gas mark 4). Then place the turkey on a serving dish. Pour the wine into the cooking dish and stir in the cooking juices. Strain the sauce through a sieve and pour into a small saucepan.
6. Discard the vegetables from the cooking dish. Bring the sauce to the boil, and boil until reduced by half. Add the cream, stir well and leave to reduce once more by half.
7. Wash the bilberries or cranberries (if fresh ones) or strain them (if using preserved ones). Add to the sauce and boil for 1 minute. Pour the sauce into a sauceboat.
8. Serve the turkey, handing the sauce separately.

Bilberries or cranberries may be replaced by fresh red or white currants.

With a jointed chicken or turkey you can prepare two different dishes. You can sauté the chicken or turkey breasts, having cut them into thin slices (or escalopes), or roll them around a savoury filling (they are then known as paupiettes*).*

With the remaining joints, prepare a fricassée *(brown the meat in butter or oil, add some stock, cover, and leave to cook).*

Rôti de Dindonneau aux Saucisses

Turkey Roast with Sausages

Serves 6.
Preparation and cooking: 1 hr 20 min
★

- ○ **1 young 1.2kg (2½ lb) turkey**
- ○ **50g (2 oz) butter**
- ○ **3 medium-sized onions**
- ○ **300g (11 oz) button mushrooms**
- ○ **3 chipolata sausages**
- ○ **150ml (¼ pint) dry white wine**
- ○ **125g (4 oz) cream**
- ○ **salt and pepper**

1. Rub the turkey with salt and pepper. Melt the butter in a flameproof casserole and brown the turkey on both sides. Cover the casserole and continue cooking for 45 minutes over a very low heat. Do not add any water during the cooking unless it sticks.
2. Meanwhile, peel and finely slice the onions. Trim and wash the mushrooms and drain. Remove the skin from the sausages and cut into slices.
3. When the roast is cooked, remove from the casserole and keep warm. Put the onions in the casserole and gently sauté over a low heat, then add the sausage slices and fry until lightly brown.
4. Cut the mushrooms into strips and add to the casserole. Sauté until they have exuded all their juice, then pour in the wine.
5. When the wine has completely evaporated, add the cream, stir well and boil for 1 minute. Turn off the heat.
6. Cut the turkey roast into slices and place on a warm serving dish. Pour the sauce over and serve at once.

Serve with small peas or fresh spinach.

Dinde au Jus de Grenade

Turkey with Pomegranate Juice

Serves 4. Preparation: 10 min Cooking: 1 hr 30 min
★

- ○ **900g (2 lb) of turkey, legs and breasts, cut into 8 pieces**
- ○ **8 thin slices of lean bacon**
- ○ **50g (2 oz) butter**
- ○ **8 fresh sage leaves**
- ○ **3 bay leaves**
- ○ **salt and pepper**
- ○ **3 ripe pomegranates**

1. Preheat the oven to 200°C (400°F; gas mark 6). Grease an ovenproof dish large enough to contain all the turkey pieces.
2. Place a sage leaf on each piece of turkey. Season with a little salt and pepper. Roll up each piece of turkey in a slice of bacon and secure with a piece of string.
3. Place the rolled turkey pieces in the cooking dish. Cut each bay leaf in half and place in between each turkey roll.
4. Cook in the oven for 45 minutes, basting frequently with the cooking juices.
5. Peel the rind from two pomegranates. Put the seeds into a vegetable mill and pass through the fine mesh of the mill. Pour the juice into the cooking dish.
6. Reduce the heat to 190°C (370°F; gas mark 5) and continue cooking for 45 minutes, basting frequently. When the cooking is over, remove the string and place the turkey pieces on a serving dish. If necessary, add a little water to the sauce in the cooking dish, stir well and pour the sauce over the turkey.
7. Peel the third pomegranate and scoop out the seeds. Garnish the dish with the seeds and serve.

The pomegranate juice may be replaced by the juice of green grapes.

Why not try one of these turkey recipes as an alternative to the traditional roast at Christmas.

Pintade aux Choux

Serves 4. Preparation: 15 min Cooking: 1 hr 45 min

Braised Guinea Fowl with Cabbage   ★★

- ○ 1 1.5kg (3 lb) guinea fowl
- ○ 2 medium-sized savoy cabbages
- ○ 1 carrot
- ○ 1 onion
- ○ 1 clove
- ○ 150g (5 oz) bacon, fatty and slightly salted
- ○ 1 sprig thyme
- ○ 1 bay leaf
- ○ ½ litre (1 pint) chicken stock
- ○ 30ml (2 tbls) goose fat or dripping
- ○ salt and pepper

1. Rub the inside of the guinea fowl with salt and pepper. Cut the cabbages into 4. Remove the hard centre stalk and coarse outer leaves. Wash well. Bring some salted water to the boil in a large saucepan. Blanch the cabbage for 3 minutes then drain and cut into strips 1cm (½ inch) wide.
2. Peel the onion and carrot. Spike the onion with a clove. Slice the carrot and cut the bacon into strips.
3. Melt the goose fat or dripping in a flameproof casserole large enough to contain the bird and vegetables, and brown the guinea fowl on all sides. Then add the bacon strips, onion, carrot, cabbage, thyme and bay leaf. Pour enough stock into the casserole to half cover the guinea fowl. Season. Cover with a lid and cook for 1 hour 30 minutes over a very low heat.
4. When the guinea fowl is cooked, place on a serving dish and surround with the cabbage. Serve at once.

To complete this dish, you may add small new potatoes to the casserole, 30 minutes before the end of cooking time. And to give an original touch, add a small saveloy, known in France as *cervelas*.

Pintadeau Braisé au Madère

Serves 4. Preparation: 10 min Cooking: 1 hr 10 min

Braised Guinea Fowl with Madeira Wine   ★★

- ○ 1 young 1.2kg (2½ lb) guinea fowl
- ○ 2 sprigs tarragon
- ○ 1 thin slice of fatty bacon, about 100g (4 oz)
- ○ 60ml (2 fl oz) cognac
- ○ 150ml (¼ pint) Madeira
- ○ 80g (3 oz) butter
- ○ 30ml (2 tbls) oil
- ○ salt and pepper

1. Rub the inside of the guinea fowl with salt and pepper. Place the sprigs of tarragon inside the bird and secure the vent with a small skewer.
2. Cover the guinea fowl breast with the bacon and secure with a piece of string.
3. Heat the oil in a flameproof casserole. Add 30g (1 oz) of butter and brown the guinea fowl on both sides over a medium heat. Cover with a lid and simmer over a low heat for 30 minutes.
4. Remove the guinea fowl from the casserole and discard the bacon and cooking fat. Put the bird back into the casserole, pour in the cognac and set alight. Then add the Madeira, salt and pepper and continue cooking for another 30 minutes, turning the bird from time to time.
5. When the bird is cooked, remove from the casserole and place on a serving dish. Keep warm.
6. Turn the heat off. Add the remaining butter to the casserole and fold in the cooking juices, beating with a whisk, to obtain a creamy sauce.
7. Pour the sauce over the guinea fowl and serve at once.

Serve this dish with mushrooms (*girolles* or *cèpes*) sautéed in butter or morels with cream.

A fowl is trussed to give it a regular shape which will be held in place during cooking. You can buy a chicken which has already been trussed by the butcher, but if you have to do it yourself, use a trussing needle threaded with a strong piece of string (or thread). Pass the needle through the right leg, then through the body and bring out through the left leg. Secure the string with a knot. Then draw the loose skin from the neck over the back. Pass the needle through the right wing, through the body and through the left wing, taking up the skin from the neck at the same time. Tie off the string.

Pintade au Cognac

Guinea Fowl with Cognac

Serves 4. Preparation: 10 min Cooking: 1 hr 10 min

★

- ○ 1 1.2kg (2½ lb) guinea fowl
- ○ 3 fresh sage leaves
- ○ 1 sprig rosemary
- ○ 3 cloves garlic, unpeeled
- ○ 4 thin slices smoked streaky bacon
- ○ 1 chicken stock cube
- ○ ¼ litre (9 fl oz) warm water
- ○ 100ml (3½ fl oz) cognac
- ○ 60ml (2 tbls) oil
- ○ 40g (1½ oz) butter
- ○ salt and pepper

1. Rub the inside of the guinea fowl with salt and pepper. Place the sage leaves inside the bird, together with the unpeeled garlic and sprig of rosemary. Sew the vent with a needle and thread or secure with a skewer.
2. Cover the breast of the guinea fowl with the bacon and secure with a piece of string.
3. Dissolve the chicken stock cube in warm water.
4. Heat the oil in a flameproof casserole, add the butter and brown the guinea fowl on both sides. Then pour in the cognac and set alight.
5. Pour in the chicken stock and season. Cover the casserole and simmer over a low heat for 30 minutes.
6. Remove the guinea fowl from the casserole, discard the bacon and string, and put the bird back in the casserole for another 30 minutes. Reserve the bacon slices.
7. 5 minutes before the cooking time is up, put the bacon back into the casserole. Then place the guinea fowl on a serving dish, with the bacon slices on top.

This dish goes well with mushrooms sautéed in butter.

Pintade aux Cerises

Guinea Fowl with Cherries

Serves 4. Preparation and cooking: 1 hr 15 min

★

- ○ 1 1.2kg (2½ lb) guinea fowl
- ○ 45ml (3 tbls) oil
- ○ 60g (2½ oz) butter
- ○ 500g (slightly over 1 lb) cherries
- ○ 2 pinches cinnamon
- ○ salt and pepper
- ○ 60ml (2 fl oz) sherry

1. Heat the oil in a flameproof casserole. Add half the butter and brown the guinea fowl on both sides. Then add 45ml (3 tbls) water, season, cover the casserole and simmer over a very low heat for 1 hour, turning the bird two or three times during the cooking.
2. Meanwhile, stone the cherries.
3. When the guinea fowl is cooked, remove from the casserole and place on a serving dish. Skim the fat off the cooking juices and put the cherries in the casserole with the remaining butter and cinnamon.
4. Carve the guinea fowl into 8 pieces, put the joints back into the casserole (with their juice) and simmer together with the cherries for 5 minutes.
5. Season. Pour in the sherry and set alight. Place on a serving dish and serve at once.

To poach does not mean to boil. The liquid used for poaching (water, stock or court-bouillon) must simmer very slowly, with only the barest movement on the surface of the liquid.

When poaching a fowl, put the head, feet and wings into the stock as well — it will improve the flavour.

If you want to serve a perfectly white poached fowl, rub the breast with half a lemon then cover it immediately with a thin slice of larding fat; secure it with string and poach the fowl.

The most delicate, and famous, way of poaching a fowl is to enclose it (stuffed, trussed and covered with larding fat) in a pork bladder which is then tied up with a piece of string. The fowl is cooked over a low heat, totally covered with stock. If you want to serve it cold, leave it to cool in the pork bladder.

Pintade Farcie aux Olives Noires
Guinea Fowl with Black Olive Stuffing

Serves 4. Preparation: 30 min
Cooking: 1 hr 10 min
★ ★ ★

- 1 1.2kg (2½ lb) guinea fowl
- the guinea fowl liver
- 250g (9 oz) button mushrooms
- 150g (5 oz) black olives
- 100g (4 oz) pork sausagemeat
- 50g (2 oz) bread, without crusts
- 100ml (3½ fl oz) warm milk
- 1 egg
- 1 chicken stock cube
- ¼ litre (9 fl oz) boiling water
- 60ml (4 tbls) oil
- 80g (3 oz) butter
- salt and pepper

1. Dissolve the chicken stock cube in the boiling water. Stone the olives and quarter them. Dice the guinea fowl liver; trim, wash and dry the mushrooms; cut them into thin strips.
2. Melt 20g (1 oz) of butter in a frying pan and sauté the mushrooms until golden; add the pork sausagemeat and mix it into the mushrooms with a fork. Add the liver, let it brown gently then remove the frying pan from the heat.
3. Soak the bread in warm milk. Put into a bowl and mash with a fork; then add the contents of the frying pan, together with the olives. Mix all ingredients well and season with a little salt and pepper. Add the egg and mix once more.
4. Stuff the guinea fowl and sew up the vent, using a needle and thread.
5. Heat the oil in a flameproof casserole. Add 20g (1 oz) of butter and brown the guinea fowl on both sides; then skim off three-quarters of the cooking fat and pour in half the stock. Cover and simmer over a low heat for 1 hour, turning the bird from time to time and basting it with the cooking juices.
6. When the guinea fowl is cooked, remove from the casserole and place on a serving dish.
7. Add the remaining butter to the casserole, beating it into the cooking juices with a whisk to obtain a smooth sauce. Pour the sauce over the guinea fowl and serve at once.

Serve with fresh spinach or any other green vegetables in season.

Pintade aux Pommes Vertes
Guinea Fowl with Apples

Serves 4. Preparation and cooking: 1 hr 15 min
★

- 1 1.2kg (2½ lb) guinea fowl, cut into 8 pieces
- 60g (2½ oz) butter
- 4 medium-sized onions, thinly sliced
- 4 green apples (cooking apples)
- salt and pepper

1. Melt half the butter in a frying pan and sauté the guinea fowl pieces over a low heat, then remove from the pan and reserve.
2. Sauté the onions over a low heat until golden, stirring frequently.
3. Put the guinea fowl pieces back into the frying pan, season and pour over 100ml (3½ fl oz) water. Cover and simmer for 45 minutes, adding a little more water during the cooking, if necessary.
4. 15 minutes before the end of the cooking time, peel, core and halve the apples. Cut each half apple into 4.
5. Melt the remaining butter in a frying pan and gently sauté the apples until they start to turn brown. Then add to the guinea fowl and simmer for 10 minutes. Serve at once.

Pintade à la Brésilienne

Serves 4. Preparation and cooking: 1 hr 20 min

Guinea Fowl Brazilian-Style

★ ★ ★

- ○ 1 1.2kg (2½ lb) guinea fowl, cut into 4 pieces
- ○ 1 large onion
- ○ 45ml (3 tbls) groundnut oil
- ○ 1 chicken stock cube
- ○ ½ litre (1 pint) boiling water
- ○ 2 cooking apples (or green apples)
- ○ 30ml (2 tbls) curry powder
- ○ 60ml (4 tbls) concentrated milk, unsweetened
- ○ 10ml (2 tsp) cornflour
- ○ 15ml (1 tbls) honey
- ○ 100g (4 oz) cream
- ○ 30ml (2 tbls) sultanas
- ○ 30ml (2 tbls) almonds, flaked and grilled
- ○ 1 green banana
- ○ juice of ½ lemon
- ○ salt and pepper

1. Dissolve the chicken stock cube in the boiling water. Soak the sultanas in warm water. Peel and finely chop the onion.
2. Heat the oil in a flameproof casserole. Brown the guinea fowl on both sides over a high heat, then add the chopped onion and sauté until golden, stirring continuously.
3. When the onion has taken on a golden colour sprinkle in the curry powder, mix well and pour in the stock. Then peel the apples and cut into 4; remove the core and pips and dice; add to the ingredients in the casserole. Cover with a lid.
4. Simmer over a low heat for 40 minutes, turning the guinea fowl from time to time.
5. Remove the guinea fowl pieces from the casserole and reserve. Mix the cornflour with cold milk and add to the casserole. Season with a very little salt (the stock is already salted) and pepper. Add the honey and mix well. Simmer over a low heat for 10 minutes, uncovered, turning the meat from time to time.
6. Meanwhile, remove the bones from the guinea fowl and discard them. Put the meat back into the casserole and add the cream. Simmer for a further 5 minutes.
7. Peel and slice the banana and pour the lemon juice over it to prevent it from turning black. Drain the sultanas.
8. Place the guinea fowl and sauce on a serving dish and garnish with the sliced banana and sultanas. Sprinkle with almonds, and serve at once.

Serve with boiled rice.

Pintade aux Poireaux

Serves 4. Preparation: 10 min Cooking: 1 hr 20 min

Guinea Fowl with Leeks

★

- ○ 1 1.2kg (2½ lb) guinea fowl, cut into 8 pieces
- ○ 50g (2 oz) butter
- ○ 100g (4 oz) smoked streaky bacon
- ○ 8 large leeks
- ○ 5ml (1 tsp) curry powder
- ○ 1 bay leaf
- ○ salt

1. Cut the bacon into thin strips.
2. Wash the leeks and discard the green part. Cut the white of the leeks into thin slices and reserve.
3. Melt the butter in a flameproof casserole over a very low heat; add the bacon and guinea fowl pieces and brown gently, turning them all the time. Season with salt.
4. Add the leeks and bay leaf to the casserole, mix well for 5 minutes, then sprinkle in the curry powder. Mix once more.
5. Cover and simmer over a low heat for 1 hour, turning the guinea fowl and leeks from time to time. The liquid from the leeks should provide enough cooking juices, but if the ingredients start to dry up or stick to the casserole, add one or two tablespoons of water.
6. Serve very hot.

Pintade aux Marrons Glacés

Serves 4. Preparation: 15 min Cooking: 1 hr 15 min

Guinea Fowl with Marrons Glacés

★

○ **1 good-sized oven-ready guinea fowl**
○ **300g (11 oz) pieces of marrons glacés (candied chestnuts)**
○ **30ml (2 tbls) double cream**
○ **45ml (3 tbls) armagnac**
○ **4 slices raw ham (eg Parma ham)**
○ **10ml (2 tsp) rosemary**
○ **salt and pepper**
○ **50g (2 oz) butter**
○ **1 chicken stock cube**
○ **150ml (¼ pint) warm water**

1. Mix the pieces of marrons glacés with the cream and 15ml (1 tbls) of armagnac.
2. Rub the inside of the guinea fowl with salt and pepper. Stuff the bird with the chestnut, cream, and armagnac mixture and sew up the vent with a needle and thread.
3. Put the rosemary into a bowl and add 2ml (½ tsp) of salt and the same amount of pepper. Mix well and spread on a board. Roll the guinea fowl in this seasoning and then cover it with the slices of ham, tying them in place with a piece of string.
4. Preheat the oven to 220°C (425°F; gas mark 7). Dissolve the chicken stock cube in a small saucepan.
5. Melt the butter over a low heat in an ovenproof casserole large enough to contain the fowl. Gently brown the guinea fowl for 10 minutes, then pour over 30ml (2 tbls) of armagnac and set alight.
6. Place the casserole in the oven and cook for about 1 hour, basting the guinea fowl with stock every 10 minutes.
7. When the guinea fowl is cooked, remove the string and cut into 4 pieces. Place some stuffing on top of each quarter, with a slice of ham underneath. Serve at once.

To accompany this dish try a green salad, such as chicory, corn salad, or endive, seasoned with French dressing.

Pintade d'Hiver

Serves 4. Preparation: 15 min Cooking: 1 hr 30 min

Guinea Fowl with Prunes and Chestnuts

★ ★

○ **1 1.2kg (2½ lb) guinea fowl**
○ **12 chestnuts**
○ **12 prunes**
○ **100g (4 oz) ham**
○ **100g (4 oz) smoked streaky bacon**
○ **50g (2 oz) butter**
○ **1 litre (1¾ pints) milk**
○ **salt**

1. Soak the prunes in warm water for 2 hours before preparing the guinea fowl.
2. After 2 hours drain the prunes, chop the ham and cut the bacon into thin strips.
3. Rub the inside of the guinea fowl with salt, then stuff with the chestnuts, prunes, chopped ham and strips of bacon. Sew the vent with a needle and thread.
4. Generously grease the bottom and sides of a flameproof casserole and put in the guinea fowl. Add the milk, which should just about cover it, and season with salt.
5. Stand the casserole on an asbestos mat and cook over a very low heat for 1 hour 30 minutes, in the simmering milk.
6. Remove the guinea fowl from the casserole and place on a serving dish. Cut it into 4 pieces and put some stuffing on top of each quarter.
7. Reduce the sauce, if necessary, by boiling it for a few minutes. When ready, it should look like golden clotted cream.
8. Pour the sauce over each quarter of guinea fowl and serve at once.

A fowl with stuffing need not cook any longer than a fowl without stuffing. Ingredients for the stuffing which are not finely chopped require more time to cook; it is therefore necessary to cook (eg fry) onions, strips of bacon, shallots, chestnuts, before they are mixed with the remaining ingredients for the stuffing.

A stuffing which is made of a mixture of egg and bread (amongst other ingredients) swells during cooking; therefore you will only need a small amount of stuffing for the fowl.

Canard Braisé aux Olives (p48) ▶

Canard Braisé aux Olives

Braised Duck with Olives

Serves 4. Preparation and cooking: 1 hr 20 min

★★

○ 1 1.6kg (3½ lb) duck
○ 1 medium-sized onion
○ 150g (5 oz) green olives, stoned
○ 150ml (5 fl oz) dry white wine
○ 20 sprigs parsley
○ 15ml (1 tbls) capers
○ the duck liver
○ 30ml (2 tbls) oil
○ 20g (¾ oz) butter
○ salt and pepper

1. Peel and finely chop the onion. Rub the inside of the duck with salt and pepper.
2. Heat the oil in a flameproof casserole, brown the duck on both sides and reserve.
3. Pour away the cooking fat and replace with the butter. When the butter has melted, put in the onion and gently sauté until slightly golden; pour in the wine and put the duck back into the casserole. Season with salt and pepper. Cover and cook over a low heat for 1 hour 10 minutes, turning the duck from time to time.
4. 15 minutes before the end of cooking time, coarsely chop the parsley; drain and chop the capers and chop the duck liver.
5. 10 minutes before the end of cooking time add the parsley, capers, duck liver and olives to the casserole. Simmer for 10 minutes.
6. When cooked place the duck on a serving dish, arrange the garnish around the duck and serve immediately.

Canard Farci aux Pignons

Duck with Pine Kernel Stuffing

Serves 4. Preparation: 20 min Cooking: 1 hr 20 min

★★★

○ 1 1.6kg (3½ lb) duck
○ 100g (4 oz) pine kernels
○ 150g (6 oz) *fromage blanc* (or very soft cream cheese)
○ 50g (2 oz) grated Gruyère
○ the duck liver
○ 100g (4 oz) chopped ham
○ 60ml (4 tbls) chopped chervil
○ 50g (2 oz) bread, without crusts
○ 30ml (2 tbls) Madeira
○ 1 egg
○ 100g (4 oz) larding fat (fresh fat back)
○ 15ml (1 tbls) oil
○ salt, pepper, nutmeg and *quatre épices* or mixed spice

1. Pour the Madeira into a bowl, add the bread and mash it with a fork. Add the *fromage blanc* and mix with the bread. Finely dice the duck liver and mix with the bread and cheese mixture, together with the ham, Gruyère and chervil. Season with salt, pepper and grated nutmeg. Add one pinch of *quatre épices* (or mixed spice) and the egg. Mix all the ingredients well, then add the pine kernels and mix once more.
2. Fill the duck with this stuffing and sew up the vent with a needle and thread.
3. Preheat the oven to 200°C (400°F; gas mark 6). Grease an ovenproof dish. Place the larding fat on the duck's breast and secure with string. Put the duck in the dish and cook in the oven for 40 minutes.
4. Remove the dish from the oven, discard the larding fat and pour away the cooking fat. Pour in 60ml (4 tbls) of water. Put the duck back into the dish, reduce the heat to 190°C (375°F; gas mark 5) and cook for 30 minutes more, basting the duck frequently with the cooking juices and adding a little water if the juices start to brown.
5. When the cooking is over, prick the duck with a fork; if the juice which spurts out is transparent, the duck is cooked, but if it is slightly pink continue cooking for a few more minutes.
6. When the duck is cooked, place on a board and carve, trying not to break the stuffing. Slice the stuffing and arrange round the duck on a serving dish. Deglaze the cooking juices with a little water and pour over the duck. Serve immediately.

To accompany this dish we suggest a green salad, such as corn salad or endive, or a fine vegetable purée.

Caneton sur Canapés de Foie

Serves 2. Preparation and cooking: 1 hr 5 min

Duckling on Liver Canapés

★★

○ **1 800g (1½ lb) duckling**
○ **the duckling liver**
○ **2 finely chopped shallots**
○ **100g (4 oz) butter**
○ **150ml (¼ pint) dry white wine**
○ **salt and pepper**
○ **2 large slices white bread**

1. Rub the inside of the duckling with salt and pepper. Melt 30g (1¼ oz) of butter in a sauté pan and brown the duckling on both sides. Season with salt and pepper, cover and simmer for 45 minutes. The duckling should be well browned on the outside but its flesh should still be slightly pink.
2. 15 minutes before the end of the cooking time, toast the slices of bread. Melt 20g (¾ oz) butter in a small frying pan and gently sauté the shallots. Add the liver and sauté for a few minutes: it should still be pink. Remove the frying pan from the heat, season with salt and pepper and blend the ingredients in an electric blender, or mash well with a fork. Add 30g (1¼ oz) of butter to this purée and mix well. Spread this mixture on to the slices of bread and put in the oven for 5 minutes at 180°C (350°F; gas mark 4).
3. When the duckling is cooked split it in half and place each half on one slice of bread.
4. Skim the fat off the sauté pan, pour in the wine and reduce by half. Remove from the heat and add the 20g (¾ oz) remaining butter. Mix with a fork and pour the sauce over the canapés. Serve immediately.

Caneton aux Haricots Blancs Frais

Serves 4. Preparation: 15 min
Cooking: 1 hr 30 min

Duckling with Fresh Haricot Beans

★★

○ **1 1.5kg (3¼ lb) duckling, cut into 8 pieces**
○ **1kg (2½ lb) fresh haricot beans**
○ **100g (4 oz) streaky bacon**
○ **1 medium-sized onion**
○ **15ml (1 tbls) tomato purée**
○ **1 bouquet garni: 1 sprig thyme, 1 bay leaf, 6 sprigs parsley**
○ **30ml (2 tbls) goose fat or oil**
○ **2ml (½ tsp) sugar**
○ **salt and pepper**

1. Shell the haricot beans (if fresh ones). Peel and chop the onion. Cut the bacon into strips.
2. Melt the goose fat (or oil) in a flameproof casserole. Quickly sauté the duck pieces over a medium heat, then remove from the casserole and reserve.
3. Put the onion and bacon into the casserole and sauté until slightly golden. Mix the tomato purée with a glass of cold water and pour into the casserole, adding at the same time the sugar and bouquet garni. Add the haricot beans and place the duck pieces on top. Season. Cover with cold water up to the level of the duck.
4. Cover the casserole and simmer over a low heat for 1 hour 10 minutes or more until the haricot beans are tender. Add more water during the cooking if necessary.
5. Serve very hot, in the cooking dish.

How to roast a fowl well in the oven. First rub the inside of the fowl with salt and pepper. Do not rub the outside with salt, because it would be dissolved into the cooking juices or fat which are used for basting the fowl and would make it too salty. Lightly grease the outside of the fowl (with butter or oil) and cook in a fairly hot oven. When the bird has turned golden reduce the heat progressively until the end of the cooking time. Start basting the fowl only during the last quarter of the cooking time, because basting causes the skin to swell up in large ugly-looking blisters. If you like the skin to be crispy only baste the fowl a little. If you like the flesh to melt in your mouth, baste it frequently.

When roasting a large fowl first place some slices of larding fat on the breast or cover with foil or greaseproof paper for the first two thirds of the cooking time. Then remove the larding fat or foil to allow the fowl to brown. If you follow these instructions, the flesh of the fowl should not be too dry.

Canard à l'Orange

Duck with Orange Sauce

Serves 4. Preparation and cooking: 1 hr 20 min

★ ★ ★

- ○ 1 1.6kg (3½ lb) duck
- ○ 6 oranges
- ○ 2 lemons
- ○ 100g (4 oz) sugar
- ○ 60ml (2 fl oz) wine vinegar
- ○ 100ml (3½ fl oz) dry white wine
- ○ 5ml (1 tsp) cornflour
- ○ 60ml (4 tbls) curaçao
- ○ 30ml (2 tbls) kummel
- ○ 15ml (1 tbls) redcurrant jelly
- ○ salt and pepper
- ○ 15ml (1 tbls) oil

1. Preheat the oven to 220°C (425°F; gas mark 7).
2. Rub the inside of the duck with salt and pepper. Grease the outside with a little oil. Grease an ovenproof dish and place the duck in it. Cook in the oven for one hour. If the cooking juices start to brown during cooking, add some water to the dish.
3. Meanwhile, prepare the fruit. Peel 2 oranges and 1 lemon, cutting off the skin but leaving the white membrane. Cut the peel into thin strips. Bring some water to the boil and blanch the strips of peel for 3 minutes, drain and reserve. Squeeze the juice from the peeled oranges and lemon and mix together.
4. Peel the remaining 4 oranges and the lemon. Cut one orange into thin slices for garnish and the other 3 oranges and the lemon into segments.
5. Put the sugar and 30ml (2 tbls) of water into a saucepan. Cook over a medium heat until the sugar starts to caramelize, then add the vinegar and the orange and lemon juice. Boil for 1 minute, stirring with a spatula to dissolve the caramelized sugar, then turn the heat off.
6. When the duck is cooked pour the juice from the inside of the duck into the cooking juices. Place the duck on a serving dish and season with salt. Cover with a sheet of greaseproof paper or foil and keep warm.
7. Skim off the fat from the cooking dish, and place it over a medium heat. Pour in the white wine and scrape the coagulated cooking juices into it. Reduce the sauce by half.
8. Mix the cornflour with the curaçao. Add this mixture to the cooking dish together with the kummel, the contents of the saucepan and the redcurrant jelly. Mix all ingredients well together. Boil this sauce for 1 minute until it thickens and the jelly melts. Then add the orange and lemon peel and the segments. Simmer for another minute and pour round the duck.
9. Garnish with the orange slices and serve immediately.

Canard au Poivre Vert

Duck with Green Pepper

Serves 4. Preparation: 5 min Cooking: 1 hr

★

- ○ 1 1.6kg (3½ lb) duck
- ○ ½ lemon
- ○ 15ml (1 tbls) green pepper
- ○ 1 sprig tarragon
- ○ salt and pepper

1. Rub the inside of the duck with salt and pepper. Place the green pepper and tarragon inside the bird and secure the vent with a skewer. Rub the skin of the duck with the half lemon and season with salt.
2. Spit roast the duck for approximately 1 hour, away from the flame. The duck should not be too well done and its flesh should be slightly pink.
3. When cooked, carve and place on a serving dish. Discard the tarragon but not the green pepper, which you eat with the duck.

Serve with a purée of turnips.

Canard en Bocal
Marinated Duck

Serves 6. Preparation: 20 min Cooking: 1 hr 10 min
To be served cold
★★

- ○ 1 1.8kg (4 lb) duck, cut into 6 pieces
- ○ 1 carrot
- ○ 1 onion
- ○ 1 celery stalk
- ○ 20 fresh sage leaves
- ○ 5ml (1 tsp) rosemary
- ○ 2 small chillies
- ○ 5ml (1 tsp) peppercorns
- ○ 4 cloves garlic, unpeeled
- ○ 15ml (1 tbls) coarse sea salt
- ○ 150ml (¼ pint) olive oil

1. Bring some water to the boil in a large saucepan. Add the sea salt. Clean and wash the vegetables and plunge them into the boiling water together with the duck pieces. Cook uncovered over a low heat for approximately 1 hour 10 minutes, or until the flesh of the duck comes away easily from the bone.
2. When the duck pieces are cooked remove from the casserole, using a slotted spoon, and leave until cool enough to remove the skin and bones.
3. Crush the unpeeled garlic with the palm of your hand. Fill a Kilner jar or preserving jar with the duck pieces in layers, placing some herbs (sage, rosemary, garlic, peppercorns etc) between each layer.
4. Pour in the olive oil to the top and seal the jar. Keep in a cool place or at the bottom of the refrigerator for 3 days. Before serving the duck, leave it for at least 2 hours at room temperature.

Serve with toast, fresh bread or bread slices rubbed with garlic.

Canard aux Olives
Duck with Olives

Serves 4. Preparation and cooking: 1 hr 40 min

- ○ 1 1.6kg (3½ lb) duck
- ○ 500g (18 oz) green olives, stoned
- ○ 80g (3 oz) butter
- ○ 20g (¾ oz) flour
- ○ ¼ litre (9 fl oz) chicken stock
- ○ 200ml (7 fl oz) Madeira
- ○ salt and pepper

1. Melt half the butter in a flameproof casserole and brown the duck on both sides, then remove from the casserole and reserve.
2. Sprinkle the flour into the casserole and stir with a spatula until slightly golden. Add the stock and Madeira, a little at a time, and bring to the boil. Put the duck back into the casserole. Season, cover and simmer over a low heat for 1 hour 15 minutes.
3. 30 minutes before the end of cooking time, bring some water to the boil in a large saucepan. Blanch the olives for 5 minutes in boiling water, drain and add to the casserole.
4. When the duck is cooked, place on a serving dish and arrange the olives around it. Reduce the cooking juices to a ¼ litre (9 fl oz) then remove the casserole from heat and beat in the remaining butter with a whisk. Pour the sauce over the duck and serve at once.

Serve with small boiled potatoes.

In the country districts of France every part of a fowl is used in cooking: the feet are cooked in water to make stock, the wings and neck are cooked in stews, and the liver is chopped and used for stuffings. Nothing goes to waste. As for the blood, it is mixed with vinegar (to prevent it from coagulating), kept until the fowl is cooked, and then used to thicken the sauce, if it is a wine sauce. The gizzard, liver, heart and neck of a fowl are known as giblets.

Canard Braisé Sauce Bigarade

Serves 4. Preparation and cooking: 1 hr 30 min

Braised Duck with Bigarade Sauce

★ ★ ★

- ◯ 1 1.5kg (3 lb) duck
- ◯ 6 oranges
- ◯ 1 carrot
- ◯ 1 onion
- ◯ 1 celery stalk
- ◯ 1 bouquet garni: 1 sprig thyme, 1 bay leaf, 4 sprigs parsley
- ◯ 150ml (¼ pint) dry white wine
- ◯ 30ml (2 tbls) oil
- ◯ 20g (¾ oz) butter
- ◯ salt and pepper
- ◯ 30ml (2 tbls) caramel
- ◯ 15ml (1 tbls) vinegar
- ◯ 5ml (1 tsp) cornflour
- ◯ 15ml (1 tbls) curacao

1. Finely peel one orange, leaving the white membrane around the orange. Cut the peel into thin strips and reserve. Cut the peeled orange into 4 pieces and place inside the duck. Secure the vent with a skewer.
2. Wash the carrot, onion and celery, peel and cut into slices.
3. Heat the oil in a flameproof casserole, add the butter and brown the duck all over together with the vegetables, over a low heat. Pour on the white wine, add the bouquet garni and cover the casserole. Simmer over a low heat for 1 hour, turning the duck from time to time.
4. 15 minutes before the end of the cooking time, blanch the strips of peel in boiling water for 5 minutes. Drain and reserve. Squeeze the juice from 3 oranges and reserve. Peel the 2 remaining oranges and cut them into segments. Reserve.
5. Mix the caramel and vinegar in a saucepan; add the orange juice and stir in the cornflour.
6. When the duck is cooked, remove from the casserole and place on a serving dish. Remove the skewer and the orange pieces. Keep the duck warm.
7. Pour the contents of the saucepan into the cooking dish. Leave the sauce to thicken by boiling it for 2 minutes, then turn the heat off and add the curacao. Mix well, sieve and pour the sauce over the duck.
8. Garnish with orange segments and peel strips. Serve immediately.

Caneton à la Normande

Serves 4. Preparation and cooking: 1 hr 25 min

Duckling Normandy-Style

★

- ◯ 1 1.5kg (3¼ lb) duckling
- ◯ 150ml (¼ pint) Muscadet
- ◯ 60ml (2 fl oz) calvados
- ◯ 200g (7 oz) cream
- ◯ 60g (2½ oz) butter
- ◯ 30ml (2 tbls) oil
- ◯ salt and pepper

1. Heat the oil in a flameproof casserole. Add 25g (1 oz) of butter and brown the duckling on both sides.
2. Pour out the cooking oil from the casserole and pour in the wine; season with salt and pepper and simmer over a low heat for 1 hour, turning the bird frequently.
3. When the duckling is cooked, place on a serving dish and keep warm. Reduce the cooking juice by more than half by boiling over a high heat; then add the calvados and cream. Stir well and boil until the sauce again reduces by half. Remove from the heat.
4. Away from the heat, add the remaining butter to the casserole and blend into the sauce, beating vigorously.
5. Carve the duckling and pour over the sauce. Serve at once.

Apples, sautéed in butter or caramelized, accompany this dish perfectly.

Before using green olives in a sauce or in a stuffing, blanch them for 5 minutes in boiling water. This removes their bitterness and enhances their delicate flavour.

Canard à l'Ananas
Duck with Pineapple

Serves 4. Preparation: 10 min Cooking: 1 hr 10 min

★★

- ○ 1 1.5kg (3½ lb) duck
- ○ 1 carrot
- ○ 1 onion
- ○ 1 celery stalk
- ○ 1 sprig thyme
- ○ 1 bay leaf
- ○ 1 pineapple
- ○ 60ml (2 fl oz) kirsch
- ○ 15ml (1 tbls) wine vinegar
- ○ 100ml (3½ fl oz) dry white wine
- ○ salt and pepper
- ○ 15ml (1 tbls) oil

1. Preheat the oven to 220°C (425°F; gas mark 7). Peel the vegetables and cut into thin strips. Rub the duck with oil and grease an ovenproof dish.
2. Rub the inside of the duck with salt and pepper. Place in the oven dish with the vegetable strips around. Add the thyme, bay leaf and 100ml (3½ fl oz) water. Put in the oven and cook for 1 hour, basting the duck frequently. Add more water if the vegetables start to dry up.
3. Meanwhile, prepare the pineapple: slice off the leaf end and cut off the skin, using a sharp knife; then cut into slices 5cm (¼ inch) thick. Place the pineapple slices in a bowl and pour over the kirsch.
4. When the duck is cooked, lift out onto a cooking dish, reserving the cooking liquid. Season the duck with salt, cover with foil and keep warm in the oven (turned off).
5. Place the cooking dish (if flameproof) over a low heat. Add the white wine and reduce the sauce by half, scraping the coagulated cooking juices into the wine. Discard the thyme and bay leaf. Stir in the caramel, vinegar and pineapple slices with the kirsch. Simmer for 2 minutes then turn off the heat.
6. Garnish the duck with pineapple slices and pour the sauce over. Serve at once.

Canard aux Navets
Duck with Turnips

Serves 4. Preparation and cooking: 1 hr 20 min

★★

- ○ 1 1.4kg (3 lb) duckling
- ○ 1kg (2½ lb) turnips
- ○ 12 small onions (or pickling onions)
- ○ 100g (4 oz) butter
- ○ 10ml (2 tsp) sugar
- ○ salt and pepper

1. Peel the onions. Rub the inside of the duck with salt and pepper. Melt 50g (2 oz) of butter in a flameproof casserole and brown the duck on both sides. Add the onions and season. Cover the casserole and simmer over a low heat for 1 hour, turning the duck frequently.
2. Meanwhile, peel and wash the turnips. Drain and wipe them dry. Cut into even-shaped pieces.
3. Melt 60g (2½ oz) of butter in a sauté pan and gently sauté the turnips for 10 minutes, then add 100ml (3½ fl oz) of water. Season with salt and cover the sauté pan with a lid. Simmer over a very low heat for 20 minutes, then sprinkle in the sugar and cook for another 10 minutes, still over a low heat. Let the turnips caramelize on all sides, shaking the pan frequently.
4. When the duck is cooked, add the turnips to the casserole and simmer for 5 minutes. Then arrange the duck on a serving dish, surround with the turnips and onions, pour the cooking liquid over and serve.

When roasting a fowl, always put some herbs such as rosemary, thyme or tarragon inside the bird. Do not forget to rub the inside with salt and pepper. Instead of stuffing, you can put the liver, heart and gizzard inside it for extra flavour. You may roast it without any fat, but if you want the skin to be golden and crusty, rub it with half a lemon before placing it in the oven.

Canard Rôti à l'Anglaise
Roast Duck English-Style

Serves 4. Preparation: 30 min Cooking: 1 hr

★★★

○ 1 1.6kg (3½ lb) duck
○ 2 large onions
○ 150g (5 oz) bread, without crusts
○ 100ml (3½ fl oz) boiling milk
○ 4 sprigs fresh sage
○ 2 slices larding fat
○ 15ml (1 tbls) oil
○ salt and pepper

1. Preheat the oven to 190°C (375°F; gas mark 5). Put the onions in the oven for 20 to 30 minutes until they are tender (the blade of a knife should cut through easily). Leave them to cool and then peel and finely chop them.
2. Coarsely chop the sage leaves. Soak the bread in hot milk and mash it with a fork. Mix the bread with the onion and sage in a bowl and season with salt and pepper.
3. Stuff the duck with this mixture and sew the vent with a needle and thread.
4. Set the oven to 220°C (425°F; gas mark 7). Grease an ovenproof dish.
5. Place the larding fat around the breast and secure with string. Roast for 40 minutes, then remove the string and larding fat and cook for another 20 minutes at 200°C (400°F; gas mark 6). During the roasting add a few tablespoons of water to the cooking dish to prevent it from burning.
6. When the duck is cooked, place on a serving dish and pour the cooking juices over. Serve at once.

A purée of apples is the best accompaniment for this dish. To prepare it, cook some apple quarters in an uncovered saucepan in 100ml (3½ fl oz) water, without sugar. Then pass through the fine mesh of a vegetable mill.

Canard en Sauce Piquante
Duck with Spicy Sauce

Serves 4. Preparation: 5 min Cooking: 1 hr 45 min

★★★

○ 1 1.6kg (3½ lb) duck, cut into 10 pieces
○ 50g (2 oz) smoked streaky bacon
○ 1 clove garlic
○ 1 sprig sage (8 leaves)
○ 1 small red chilli (or hot red pepper)
○ salt
○ 45ml (3 tbls) groundnut oil
○ 150ml (¼ pint) red wine
○ 1 small tin tomato purée
○ 2 anchovy fillets in oil
○ 30ml (2 tbls) capers

1. Cut the bacon into very thin strips. Peel the garlic and chop into thin strips. Dilute the tomato purée in 100ml (3½ fl oz) warm water.
2. Heat the oil in a flameproof casserole. Brown the duck joints for 10 minutes approximately; then remove from the casserole and reserve. Pour out the cooking fat from the casserole, leaving approximately 15ml (1 tbls) at the bottom.
3. Put the bacon, garlic and sage in the casserole and gently sauté until golden. Put the duck joints back into the casserole, together with the cooking juices and the chopped chilli. Pour in the red wine and diluted tomato purée. Stir well, season with salt and cover.
4. Cook over a low heat for approximately 1 hour 30 minutes, turning the duck joints from time to time.
5. Meanwhile, drain and chop the capers together with the anchovy fillets. Add this mixture to the sauce in the casserole 5 minutes before the end of the cooking time. Mix well.

Serve very hot with boiled potatoes or polenta.

The muscovy duck is a kind of duck that likes to fly; its flesh is therefore firmer and less fatty than other farmyard ducks. Young ducklings, with tender flesh, are best roasted with delicate mixtures of fruit or new vegetables. When ducks are larger and older, they may be sautéed, or used for pâtés or galantines (a galantine is a dish of bones and stuffed poultry, game or meat, glazed with aspic and served cold).

Canard en Gelée aux Pruneaux

Serves 4. Preparation: 30 min Cooking: 1 hr 20 min
To be served cold
★ ★ ★

Jellied Duck with Prunes

- ○ 1 1.2kg (2½ lb) duck, boned, except for the legs
- ○ the duck liver
- ○ 24 large prunes
- ○ ½ litre (1 pint) warm, strong tea
- ○ 2 shallots, finely chopped
- ○ 100g (4 oz) belly of pork
- ○ 100g (4 oz) bacon
- ○ salt, pepper, mixed spice or pickling spices
- ○ 50g (2 oz) butter
- ○ 1 packet powdered gelatine
- ○ 1 lemon
- ○ 100ml (3½ fl oz) Madeira
- ○ 1 small tin of foie gras

1. Soak the prunes in tea overnight.
2. The next day boil the prunes in the tea for 10 minutes over a low heat, then drain and leave to cool. Remove the stones and reserve 8 prunes for the stuffing. Stuff each of the 16 remaining prunes with a small amount of foie gras.
3. Cut the belly of pork into strips and put in a frying pan. Sauté in butter over a low heat, together with the shallots and duck liver. When golden, remove from the heat. Cut the bacon into small pieces and add to the frying pan; add 30ml (2 tbls) of Madeira and season with salt, pepper and mixed spice to taste.
4. Turn out the contents of the frying pan onto a chopping board and chop finely. Quarter the 8 prunes and add to the mixture. Mix well, then use to stuff the duck. Sew up the vent with a needle and thread.
5. Melt the remaining butter in a flameproof casserole over a low heat and brown the duck on both sides. Season with salt and pepper; add 45ml (3 tbls) of water, cover and cook over a low heat for 1 hour, turning the duck frequently and adding a little water if necessary.
6. When the duck is cooked, place on a wire tray over a baking sheet and leave to get cold.
7. Prepare the gelatine according to the instructions on the packet, add the remaining Madeira and the lemon juice and reduce to approximately 150ml (¼ pint). Glaze the duck by brushing it over a few times with the liquid jelly.
8. Place the duck on a serving dish and surround with the prunes; pour over the remaining jelly and leave in the refrigerator until you are ready to serve.

Canard à l'Alsacienne

Serves 4. Preparation and cooking: 1 hr 35 min
★ ★

Duck Alsace-Style

- ○ 1 1.5kg (3½ lb) duck
- ○ 30ml (2 tbls) oil
- ○ 30g (1 oz) butter
- ○ ½ bottle of dry white wine (from Alsace if possible)
- ○ 600g (1¼ lb) tin of sauerkraut
- ○ 4 thick slices smoked streaky bacon
- ○ 100g (4 oz) sliced ham
- ○ salt and pepper

1. Heat the oil in a flameproof casserole. Add the butter and brown the duck on both sides, then skim off three-quarters of the cooking fat. Season with salt and pepper and pour over the wine. Simmer for 1 hour 15 minutes over a low heat, turning the duck a few times.
2. 15 minutes before the end of the cooking time, put the sauerkraut in a saucepan and warm over a low heat. Quickly grill the bacon slices on both sides and place on top of the sauerkraut. Cover to keep warm.
3. 10 minutes before the duck is ready, dice the ham finely and add to the casserole.
4. When ready, remove the duck from the casserole and place on a serving dish; surround with the sauerkraut and bacon. Reduce the cooking juices over a high heat to 100ml (3½ fl oz), pour over the duck and sauerkraut, and serve at once.

Oie en Sauce Veloutée

Goose in Cream Sauce

Serves 6-8. Preparation and cooking: 3 hr

★★★

- ○ 1 2.5kg (5½ lb) goose, with giblets
- ○ 3 carrots
- ○ 2 leeks
- ○ 1 celery stalk
- ○ 1 onion
- ○ 3 cloves
- ○ 1 whole head of garlic, unpeeled
- ○ 1 bouquet garni: 1 sprig thyme, 1 bay leaf, 10 parsley stalks
- ○ 100g (4 oz) goose fat or dripping
- ○ salt

For the sauce:
- ○ ½ litre (1 pint) milk
- ○ ½ litre (1 pint) goose stock
- ○ 1 head of garlic
- ○ 100g (4 oz) bread, without crusts
- ○ 125g (5 oz) cream
- ○ 4 egg yolks
- ○ salt and pepper

1. Peel the onion and spike with 3 cloves. Peel and wash the carrots and turnips, clean and wash the leeks. Cut each vegetable into 4 pieces. Wash the celery and cut into 2.
2. Place the goose in a very large saucepan together with the giblets. Add the carrots, turnips, leeks, celery, onion and bouquet garni. Add also the head of garlic, unpeeled. Pour in enough cold water to barely cover the goose. Bring to the boil uncovered over a low heat. Skin off the froth which appears on top, season with salt and cook for 2 hours.
3. 30 minutes before the end of the cooking time, peel the second head of garlic and cook it in milk in a saucepan over a very low heat.
4. When the goose is cooked remove from the stock, place on a board and carve into 12 pieces.
5. Melt the goose fat in a sauté pan and brown the goose pieces over a high heat until they turn golden. Drain and keep warm.
6. Pour ½ litre (1 pint) of the goose stock into a saucepan and skim the fat off. Add to the garlic and milk in the other saucepan. Crumble the bread and sprinkle into the saucepan. Boil for 5 minutes then remove from the heat. Strain this sauce through a sieve (or fine mesh of a mill) or liquidize it. Add the egg yolks and mix well, then put back on the heat, beating all the time until the sauce starts to froth. Remove from the heat before it boils and stir in the cream. Check the seasoning.
7. Place the goose pieces on a serving dish and pour over some of the sauce. Serve the rest in a sauceboat.

Serve with salsify sautéed in butter or braised celery hearts.

Oie Rôtie Sauce Myrtilles

Roast Goose with Bilberry Sauce

Serves 6. Preparation and cooking: 2 hr 40 min

- ○ 1 2.5kg (5½ lb) goose
- ○ 250g (9 oz) bilberries, or a jar of puréed bilberries
- ○ 200ml (7 fl oz) red wine
- ○ 3 pinches cinnamon
- ○ the juice of ½ lemon
- ○ salt, pepper and nutmeg

1. Preheat the oven to 200°C (400°F; gas mark 6). Rub the inside of the goose with salt and pepper. Place in an ovenproof dish and roast for 1 hour, then reduce the heat to 180°C (375°F; gas mark 5) and cook for 1 hour 30 minutes.
2. When the goose is cooked, remove from the oven, place on a serving dish and keep warm.
3. Skim the fat from the cooking juices. Pour the wine into the cooking dish and bring to the boil, then add the puréed bilberries, cinnamon, salt, pepper and grated nutmeg. Mix well and boil until the sauce reduces by half, then turn the heat off and add the lemon juice.
4. Carve the goose. Sieve the sauce and pour it over the meat. Serve immediately.

A purée of celeriac, chestnuts sautéed in butter or sautéed sweet potatoes accompany this dish very well. The purée of bilberries may be replaced by redcurrant jelly.

Oie Farcie aux Marrons

Serves 6-8. Preparation: 50 min Cooking: 2 hr 35 min

Goose with Chestnut Stuffing

★★

○ 1 2.5kg (5½ lb) goose
○ 1kg (2¼ lb) chestnuts
○ 1 celeriac
○ 1 carrot
○ 1 large onion
○ 1 celery stalk
○ 1 bay leaf
○ ½ litre (1 pint) dry white wine
○ 15ml (1 tbls) oil
○ salt and pepper

1. Peel the chestnuts. Peel the celeriac and dice it. Put some water in a large saucepan and add the chestnuts. Bring to the boil over a medium heat. After 20 minutes cooking, season with salt and add the celeriac. Boil for another 10 minutes, then drain.
2. Meanwhile, peel the carrot and onion, and cut into thin slices together with the celery stalk. Grease an ovenproof dish and place the vegetables in it, with the bay leaf.
3. Preheat the oven to 200°C (400°F; gas mark 6). Rub the inside of the goose with salt and pepper, and fill it with the chestnuts and celeriac. Sew up the vent with a needle and thread. Place in the cooking dish on the bed of vegetables and cook in the oven for 1 hour.
4. Reduce the heat to 190°C (375°F; gas mark 5) and continue cooking for another 1 hour 30 minutes, adding the wine 100ml (3½ fl oz) at a time to the cooking dish. Baste the goose with this liquid frequently.
5. When the goose is cooked, place on a serving dish. Add a little water (if necessary) to the juices and pass this sauce through a fine sieve. Skim the fat off and pour the sauce into a sauceboat. Carve the goose and place the chestnut and celeriac stuffing around the bird. Serve with the sauce in the sauceboat.

Oie Rôtie aux Pommes de Terre

Serves 6. Preparation and cooking: 2 hr

Roast Goose with Potatoes

★★

○ 1 2kg (4½ lb) goose
○ 1.5kg (3 lb) potatoes
○ 2 sprigs thyme
○ 1 tin truffles
○ salt and pepper

1. Preheat the oven to 200°C (400°F; gas mark 6). Rub the inside of the goose with salt and pepper and put the thyme inside the bird. Pour 1 glass of water into a meat tin and place the goose in the meat tin sitting on a wire rack. Cook in the oven for 30 minutes.
2. Meanwhile, peel and wash the potatoes, drain and cut them into thin slices.
3. Grease a large ovenproof dish. Arrange the potatoes as tightly as possible in layers. Season and place the strips of truffles in between each layer.
4. After 30 minutes, remove the goose from the oven and place on top of the potatoes. Remove the meat tin from the oven and pour away the water and cooking fat: at this stage, the goose has not rendered any fat. Reduce the heat to 190°C (375°F; gas mark 5) and put the goose back in the oven for 1 hour 30 minutes. The potatoes will cook and be impregnated with the fat and cooking juices from the goose. They should be cooked and flavoured to perfection.
5. When the goose is cooked, remove from the oven. Serve in the cooking dish on the bed of potatoes.

There are different ways of peeling chestnuts. The two most common are as follows: make a small cut on the flat side of the chestnuts and roast them on a baking tray in a very hot oven for 8 minutes; or, after having made a small cut on each chestnut, plunge them into very hot oil for 8 minutes.

Oie à la Viennoise

Serves 8-10. Preparation: 30 min Cooking: 3 hr

Goose Viennese-Style

★★

- ○ 1 3.5kg (7½ lb) goose
- ○ 1kg (2¼ lb) sauerkraut
- ○ 4 medium-sized onions
- ○ 2 apples (Cox's orange pippins if possible)
- ○ 2 medium-sized potatoes
- ○ 15ml (1 tbls) juniper berries
- ○ 2ml (½ tsp) cumin
- ○ 80g (3 oz) goose fat or dripping
- ○ salt and pepper

1. Peel and finely slice the onions. Wash the sauerkraut in cold water. Drain. Rub the inside of the goose with salt and pepper.
2. Melt the goose fat in a flameproof casserole and gently sauté the onions until golden. Then add the sauerkraut and cook over a medium heat for 15 minutes, uncovered, stirring frequently.
3. Peel the apples, remove the core and pips, grate and add to the sauerkraut. Season and add the cumin and juniper berries. Mix well and turn off the heat.
4. Set the oven to 190°C (375°F; gas mark 5). Stuff the goose with the contents of the casserole and sew up the vent with a needle and thread.
5. Place the goose in an ovenproof dish and cook for 1 hour 30 minutes then reduce the heat to 180°C (350°F; gas mark 4) and cook for a further 1 hour 30 minutes, basting the goose from time to time.
6. When the goose is cooked, place on a serving dish. Skim the fat from the cooking juices and deglaze with 60ml (4 tbls) water. Pour this sauce into a sauceboat.
7. Bring the whole goose to the table with the sauce in the sauceboat.

Oie Farcie aux Fruits Secs

Serves 6-8. Preparation: 15 min Cooking: 2 hr 30 min

Goose with Dried Fruit Stuffing

★★

- ○ 1 2.5kg (5½ lb) goose
- ○ 250g (9 oz) sultanas
- ○ 250g (9 oz) prunes
- ○ 250g (9 oz) dried figs
- ○ 12 shelled walnuts
- ○ 5ml (1 tsp) green pepper
- ○ 30ml (2 tbls) armagnac
- ○ 200ml (7 fl oz) dry white wine
- ○ salt and pepper

1. Wash the prunes and sultanas and soak in lukewarm water overnight.
2. The next day, drain the sultanas and prunes, remove the stones from the prunes and cut into 4. Wash and finely dice the figs. Coarsely chop the walnuts. Put all the fruit and nuts into a bowl together with the green pepper, and mix well. Pour over the armagnac and mix once more.
3. Set the oven at 200°C (400°F; gas mark 6). Rub the inside of the goose with salt and pepper and stuff the bird with the fruit mixture. Sew up the vent with a needle and thread and place the goose in an ovenproof dish.
4. Roast for 1 hour, then reduce the heat to 190°C (375°F; gas mark 5) and cook for another 1 hour 30 minutes. Pour some of the wine into the cooking dish little by little, topping it up whenever it starts to evaporate. Baste the goose from time to time.
5. When the goose is cooked, place on a serving dish. Skim the fat from the cooking juices, and pour this sauce into a sauceboat. Carve the goose.
6. Serve the carved goose, with the stuffing around it and the sauce in the sauceboat.

Fresh fruit goes very well with this dish, such as diced pineapple, sliced oranges, mangoes or bananas moistened with lemon juice, and when in season raspberries or redcurrants.

Poultry is an excellent food for diets; it contains less fat than beef, veal or lamb, its flesh is rich in protein and vitamins, it has a low calory content and it is easy to digest.

Oie Farcie aux Raisins au Rhum

Goose Stuffed with Sultanas Marinated in Rum

Serves 6-8. Preparation: 20 min
Cooking: 2 hr 30 min
★ ★

○ 1 2.5kg (5½ lb) goose
○ 6 apples (Cox's orange pippins, if possible)
○ 200g (7 oz) sultanas
○ 200ml (7 fl oz) rum
○ 3 chipolata sausages
○ 50g (2 oz) butter
○ 15ml (1 tbls) oil
○ salt and pepper

1. Soak the sultanas in lukewarm water overnight. Drain and put in a large bowl. Heat the rum gently and pour over the sultanas, leave to swell until the next day.
2. The next day, cut the apples into 4, peel and remove the core. Heat the butter in a frying pan and quickly brown the apple quarters over a brisk heat, until they start to caramelize. Turn off the heat.
3. Grill the sausages, but do not let them cook through. Cut into 4 pieces and put aside.
4. Preheat the oven to 200°C (400°F; gas mark 6). Rub the inside of the goose with salt and pepper and stuff with the apples, sausages and sultanas. Sew up the vent with a needle and thread.
5. Grease an ovenproof dish, place the goose in the cooking dish and cook for 1 hour. Then skim the fat off the cooking juices and pour in 200ml (7 fl oz) of water. Turn the heat down to 190°C (375°F; gas mark 5) and cook for a further 1 hour 30 minutes, adding more water as necessary. Baste the goose frequently.
6. When the goose is cooked, place on a serving dish. Deglaze the cooking juices with a little water and pour this sauce into a sauceboat. Serve the goose at once with the sauce in the sauceboat.

Serve with a smooth purée of chestnuts, to which you can add a little of the cooking juices just before serving.

Oie Farcie aux Reinettes

Goose with Apple Stuffing

Serves 6-8. Preparation: 15 min Cooking: 2 hr 30 min
★

○ 1 2.5kg (5½ lb) goose
○ 1kg (2½ lb) small apples (Cox's orange pippins, if possible)
○ 2 small sprigs rosemary
○ salt and pepper

1. Rub the inside of the goose with salt and pepper. Wash and wipe the apples. Remove the core using an apple corer, but do not peel them.
2. Preheat the oven to 200°C (400°F; gas mark 6). Fill the goose with the apples and rosemary. Sew up the vent with a needle and thread.
3. Place the goose into a greased ovenproof dish and roast for 1 hour, then reduce the heat to 190°C (375°F; gas mark 5) and cook for a further 1 hour 30 minutes, basting the goose occasionally. From the middle of the cooking time onwards, add a little water whenever the cooking juices start to caramelize.
4. When the goose is cooked, place on a serving dish and carve. Arrange the apples around. Skim the fat off the cooking juices and pour this sauce into a sauceboat.
5. Serve at once, with the sauce in the sauceboat.

You can serve some warm redcurrant jelly, a purée of bilberries or cranberries, or small cherries preserved in vinegar with this dish.

Up to 4kg (9 lb) a goose may be prepared in the same way as any other fowl. In France, and particularly in the Toulouse area, a goose may weigh up to 10kg (more than 20 lb) but it is used for the confit *or preserved goose and its liver is used for the famous* foie gras.

Lapin aux Poivrons (p64) ▶

Lapin aux Poivrons

Serves 4. Preparation: 15 min Cooking: 1 hr 15 min

Rabbit with Peppers

★★

- ○ 1 1.2kg (2½ lb) rabbit, cut into 8 pieces
- ○ 1 large onion
- ○ 2 cloves garlic, unpeeled
- ○ 1 green pepper
- ○ 1 yellow pepper
- ○ 1 red pepper
- ○ 1 tin 400g (14 oz) peeled tomatoes
- ○ 1 sprig thyme
- ○ 1 bay leaf
- ○ 15ml (1 tbls) chopped parsley
- ○ 60ml (4 tbls) oil
- ○ salt and pepper

1. Peel and chop the onion. Open the tomato tin and pour the tomatoes into a bowl, keeping the juice aside. Cut the tomatoes into halves and remove the seeds. Coarsely mash using a fork. Add the mashed tomatoes to the juice. Wash and cut the peppers into 4. Remove the seeds and cut into strips.
2. Heat the oil in a sauté pan and brown the rabbit pieces over a medium heat, then remove from the pan and sauté the chopped onion until golden. Add the unpeeled cloves of garlic and pepper strips. Lightly sauté all ingredients, then put the rabbit pieces back into the pan.
3. Pour in the tomato purée. Season. Add the thyme and bay leaf. Cover with a lid and simmer over a low heat for 1 hour, turning the rabbit in the sauce occasionally.
4. When the cooking time is over, check whether the rabbit is well done: the meat should come off the bones easily. Reduce the sauce in the uncovered pan and pour all ingredients into a serving dish. Sprinkle with chopped parsley and serve immediately.

Serve with boiled or jacket potatoes.

Lapin aux Pruneaux

Serves 4. Preparation and cooking: 2 hr

Rabbit with Prunes

★★

- ○ 1 1.2kg (2½ lb) rabbit, cut into 8 pieces
- ○ 100g (4 oz) streaky, smoked bacon
- ○ 20 small onions
- ○ 250g (9 oz) prunes
- ○ 15ml (1 tbls) Dijon mustard
- ○ ¼ litre (9 fl oz) dry white wine
- ○ 15ml (1 tbls) flour
- ○ 2 pinches thyme
- ○ 50g (2 oz) butter
- ○ 30ml (2 tbls) cognac
- ○ 15ml (1 tbls) liquid caramel
- ○ salt and pepper

1. The day before cooking the rabbit, or at least 2 hours before, wash and soak the prunes in lukewarm water.
2. Cut the bacon into thin strips and peel the small onions.
3. Melt the butter in a flameproof casserole over a very low heat and gently fry the bacon. Remove from the casserole and brown the rabbit joints; remove from the casserole and put in the onions. Fry until golden, still over a low heat.
4. Meanwhile, rub the rabbit pieces with the mustard. When the onions are golden put the bacon and rabbit back into the casserole. Sprinkle in the flour and stir until it starts to turn golden, then pour in the wine. Season and add the thyme. Cover with a lid and simmer for 1 hour over a low heat.
5. After an hour, add the drained prunes and the cognac. Simmer for a further 30 minutes over a low heat.
6. When the rabbit is cooked, place on a serving dish together with the prunes and onions. Pour the caramel into the casserole and mix well with the cooking juices. Pour this sauce over the rabbit and serve immediately.

Serve with a smooth purée of potatoes or chips.

The pepper (green, red or yellow) is only the sweet variety of the capsicum. Green peppers are the least sweet of the three kinds, yellow peppers are the sweetest and red peppers are also very sweet but have a nutmeg flavour. When buying peppers, make sure that their skins are smooth, firm and taut: that shows they are fresh.

Lapin sur Canapés
Rabbit on Canapés

Serves 4. Preparation: 10 min Cooking: 1 hr 10 min

★★

- ○ 1 1.2kg (2½ lb) rabbit, cut into 8 pieces
- ○ the rabbit liver
- ○ 30ml (2 tbls) flour
- ○ 100g (4 oz) butter
- ○ 30ml (2 tbls) groundnut oil
- ○ 1 medium-sized onion
- ○ 2 celery stalks, the white part only
- ○ 1 large carrot
- ○ 50g (2 oz) smoked, streaky bacon
- ○ 10 sprigs parsley
- ○ 100ml (3½ fl oz) dry white wine
- ○ 1 chicken stock cube
- ○ 200ml (7 fl oz) warm water
- ○ 20 black olives
- ○ 30ml (2 tbls) capers
- ○ 3 anchovy fillets in oil
- ○ salt and pepper
- ○ 8 slices of white bread

1. Put the flour on a plate and dip the rabbit pieces in it. Shake to remove the excess flour.
2. Peel and finely chop the onion. Peel and finely dice the carrot. Finely dice the celery and bacon. Coarsely chop the parsley.
3. Heat the oil over a low heat in a sauté pan, add 50g (2 oz) butter and brown the rabbit pieces all over. Remove and reserve.
4. Pour away most of the cooking fat, leave approximately 30ml (2 tbls) in the pan.
5. Put the bacon, vegetables and parsley in the sauté pan and cook over a low heat for 5 minutes until golden, then put the rabbit pieces back into the pan.
6. Season to taste. Pour in the wine and simmer for 10 minutes, until it has completely evaporated.
7. Dissolve the chicken stock cube in warm water and pour this stock into the sauté pan. Cover with a lid and simmer for 40 or 45 minutes, until the rabbit is well cooked and tender.
8. Meanwhile, stone the olives. Drain the capers and anchovy fillets. Chop finely, together with the rabbit liver. At the end of the cooking time, add these ingredients to the sauté pan and simmer for a further 5 minutes, stirring frequently.
9. Quickly fry the bread slices in 50g (2 oz) of butter in a frying pan and place on a serving dish. Arrange 1 rabbit piece on each slice of bread together with 15ml (1 tbls) of sauce. Serve immediately.

Lapin aux Pignons
Rabbit with Pine Kernels

Serves 4. Preparation and cooking: 1 hr 20 min

★

- ○ 4 rabbit joints
- ○ 30ml (2 tbls) oil
- ○ 20g (1 oz) butter
- ○ 100ml (3½ fl oz) cognac
- ○ 100g (4 oz) pine kernels
- ○ 250g (9 oz) cream
- ○ salt, pepper and nutmeg

1. Heat the oil in a flameproof casserole, add the butter and sauté the rabbit joints until golden. Season to taste and pour in the cognac. Turn the rabbit a few times, so that it absorbs the flavour of the cognac.
2. When the cognac has evaporated, add the cream and pine kernels. Season with grated nutmeg. Cover and simmer over a low heat for 1 hour 15 minutes. If the cream reduces too quickly while cooking, add a little water.
3. When the rabbit is cooked (the meat should come easily off the bones) place on a serving dish. Pour over the sauce with the pine kernels – it should be rather thick. Serve immediately.

Steamed or sautéed potatoes go very well with this dish.

Rabbit has a delicate flesh, but it can be rather insipid. That is why marinades with wine, or simply with oil and herbs, are a perfect way of adding more flavour.

Lapin aux Olives
Rabbit with Olives

Serves 4. Preparation: 15 min Cooking: 1 hr 15 min

★★

○ 1 1.2kg (2½ lb) rabbit, cut into 8 pieces
○ 3 medium-sized carrots
○ 2 cloves garlic
○ 1 tin 400g (14 oz) peeled tomatoes
○ 100g (4 oz) green olives, stoned
○ 100g (4 oz) black olives, stoned
○ 1 chicken stock cube
○ 2ml (½ tsp) savory
○ 30g (1 oz) butter
○ 30ml (2 tbls) oil
○ salt and pepper

1. Peel the carrots and cut into thin slices. Peel the garlic. Slice the olives. Pass the contents of the tomato tin through the fine mesh of a vegetable mill or liquidize.
2. Heat the oil in a flameproof casserole, add the butter and sauté the rabbit pieces together with the garlic and carrots, but do not let them brown. Season. Add the savory and pour in the tomato purée. Add the chicken stock cube and mash it into the sauce.
3. Cover the casserole and simmer for 1 hour over a low heat. If the sauce reduces too quickly, add a little water from time to time.
4. After 1 hour's cooking, add the olives and simmer for another 15 minutes over a very low heat.
5. When the rabbit is cooked, arrange it on a serving dish. Pour over the sauce (it should be of a thick consistency) and serve at once.

Steamed potatoes sprinkled with fresh parsley are a good accompaniment to this dish.

Lapin à la Moutarde
Rabbit with Mustard Sauce

Serves 6. Preparation: 10 min Cooking: 50 min

★★

○ 1 1.5kg (3 lb) rabbit, cut into 6 pieces
○ 45ml (3 tbls) hot mustard (Dijon type)
○ 30ml (2 tbls) groundnut oil
○ 45ml (3 tbls) dry white wine
○ 200g (7 oz) cream
○ salt and pepper

1. Set the oven to 220°C (425°F; gas mark 7). With 15ml (1 tbls) of oil grease an ovenproof dish large enough to lay all the rabbit pieces flat on the bottom.
2. Put the mustard and the remaining oil into a bowl. Season with a little salt and a lot of pepper. Mix well, beating with a fork.
3. Dip the rabbit pieces, one by one, into the mustard and arrange them in the cooking dish. Cook in the oven for 40 minutes, 30 minutes at 220°C (425°F; gas mark 7) and 10 minutes at 200°C (400°F; gas mark 6).
4. After 15 minutes, pour 30ml (2 tbls) of water into the cooking dish and baste the rabbit. Repeat the operation whenever the juices start to evaporate, using altogether approximately 200ml (7 fl oz) of water. Turn the rabbit two or three times during the cooking.
5. When the rabbit is cooked, remove from the cooking dish and place on a serving dish. Put the cooking dish (if flameproof) over the heat and pour in the wine. Scrape the cooking juices into the wine, using a spatula, until the wine evaporates, then add the cream and reduce to a third.
6. Pour this sauce over the rabbit, straining through a sieve. Serve immediately.

Serve with fresh pasta, such as tagliatelle, lightly buttered.

The best way to slice an onion finely is to peel it, and cut it into halves lengthways from top to tail; then cut it into thin slices on a board, using a very sharp knife.

If you are using fresh parsley, it is best to use the plain-leaved variety – it is tastier and has more flavour than the curly-leaved type. The latter may be fried and used for certain recipes, but it is mainly used for garnish.

Lapin à l'Espagnole

Rabbit Spanish-Style

Serves 4. Preparation: 10 min Cooking: 1 hr 20 min

★★

○ 1 1.2kg (2½ lb) rabbit, cut into 8 pieces
○ 250g (9 oz) button mushrooms
○ 100g (4 oz) stuffed green olives
○ ¼ litre (9 fl oz) dry white wine
○ 30ml (2 tbls) chopped parsley
○ 30ml (2 tbls) oil
○ 50g (2 oz) butter
○ salt and pepper
○ 4 medium-sized potatoes
○ the juice of 1 lemon

1. Trim the mushrooms. Wash, drain and cut them into 4 pieces. Sprinkle with the lemon juice.
2. Heat the oil in a sauté pan. Add the butter and brown the rabbit pieces all over. Then add the mushrooms, chopped parsley and white wine. Season, cover the pan and simmer for 1 hour 10 minutes.
3. Meanwhile, wash the potatoes. Put them into a saucepan unpeeled and cover with cold water. When the water starts to boil, cook over a low heat for 15 to 20 minutes. Check whether they are cooked or not by putting the blade of a knife through one. They should still be firm. Remove from the heat and leave to cool. Then peel and cut them into thin slices. Add to the sauté pan together with the olives and cook for 10 minutes (10 minutes before the rabbit should be ready).
4. When the rabbit is cooked, place on a serving dish, arrange the vegetables around and bring to the table.

Lapin au Lait

Rabbit in Milk Sauce

Serves 4. Preparation and cooking: 1 hr 30 min

★

○ 1 1.2kg (2½ lb) rabbit, cut into 8 pieces
○ 50g (2 oz) butter
○ 6 fresh sage leaves
○ 2ml (½ tsp) rosemary
○ ½ litre (1 pint) milk
○ salt and pepper
○ nutmeg

1. Melt the butter in a flameproof casserole over a very low heat and brown the rabbit pieces, together with the sage and rosemary. Then pour over the milk. Season with salt, pepper and grated nutmeg. Cover and simmer over a very low heat for 1 hour 15 minutes approximately.
2. At the end of the cooking time the milk will have nearly evaporated and the sauce should be a thick consistency and a golden colour. If not, reduce for a few minutes over a medium heat, turning the rabbit a few times.
3. Serve when the ingredients have taken on a golden colour.

A smooth purée of potatoes is a good accompaniment.

Lapin à la Crème

Rabbit in Cream Sauce

Serves 4. Preparation and cooking: 1 hr 30 min

★

○ 1 1.2kg (2½ lb) rabbit, cut into 8 pieces
○ 40g (1½ oz) butter
○ the juice of 1 lemon
○ 250g (9 oz) cream
○ salt and white pepper
○ nutmeg

1. Melt the butter in a flameproof casserole over a very low heat. Brown the rabbit pieces and season with salt and pepper. Pour in the lemon juice, turning the rabbit pieces over a few times, so that the flesh can absorb the lemon juice.
2. When the lemon juice has completely evaporated add the cream and grated nutmeg. Cover the casserole and simmer for 1 hour 15 minutes approximately over a very low heat, until the meat is tender and comes easily off the bones.
3. Arrange the rabbit on a serving dish and pour over the sauce, which should be of a thick consistency and of a golden colour. Serve at once.

Potatoes – steamed, sauté or chips – go very well with this dish.

Lapin au Chou

Rabbit with Cabbage

Serves 4. Preparation and cooking: 1 hr 30 min

★★

- ○ 1 1.2kg (2½ lb) rabbit, cut into 8 pieces
- ○ 1 small cabbage
- ○ 100g (4 oz) smoked, streaky bacon
- ○ 2 large onions
- ○ 250g (9 oz) Toulouse sausage or other spiced sausage
- ○ 90ml (6 tbls) oil
- ○ salt and pepper
- ○ 15ml (1 tbls) chopped parsley

1. Discard the outer leaves of the cabbage. Cut into 4 pieces, wash and cut it into thin strips.
2. Put 45ml (3 tbls) of oil in a flameproof casserole. Add the cabbage strips. Season and cover with a lid. Cook for 20 minutes over a very low heat.
3. Peel the onions and cut into thin slices. Cut the bacon into thin strips.
4. Heat 45ml (3 tbls) of oil in a sauté pan. Brown the rabbit pieces and the bacon. Season. When the ingredients are brown, remove the rabbit and bacon and reserve.
5. Gently fry the onions in the sauté pan and add the sausage. Mash it with a fork and when the onions and sausage are brown, turn off the heat.
6. Set the oven to 190°C (375°F; gas mark 5). Take an ovenproof dish large enough to lay the rabbit pieces flat on the bottom and spread some cabbage strips over it. Put the rabbit on top, together with the bacon, onions and sausage. Cover with a second layer of cabbage.
7. Cover the cooking dish tightly with two sheets of foil and cook in the oven for 1 hour.
8. Remove the dish from the oven. Discard the foil and sprinkle the rabbit with chopped parsley. Serve immediately in the cooking dish.

Lapin Vert

Rabbit with Herbs

Serves 4. Preparation and cooking: 55 min

★

- ○ 1 1.2kg (2½ lb) rabbit, cut into 8 pieces
- ○ 30ml (2 tbls) oil
- ○ 60g (2 oz) butter
- ○ 1 sprig thyme
- ○ 1 bay leaf
- ○ 2ml (½ tsp) rosemary
- ○ 20 sprigs parsley
- ○ 1 small bunch fresh chervil
- ○ 2 sprigs tarragon
- ○ 1 clove garlic
- ○ the juice of 2 lemons
- ○ salt and pepper

1. Heat the oil in a flameproof casserole. Add one knob of butter and brown the rabbit pieces, together with the thyme, bay leaf and rosemary.
2. When the rabbit pieces are brown, after approximately 20 minutes cooking, pour out the fat and sprinkle with the lemon juice. Season and cover with a lid. Simmer over a very low heat for 20 minutes approximately, until the lemon juice has evaporated.
3. Meanwhile, chop the herbs and garlic. After 40 minutes cooking time, add to the casserole together with the remaining butter and 100ml (3½ fl oz) of water. Simmer, covered, over a very low heat for 15 minutes.
4. Serve very hot.

New potatoes in their jackets go very well with this dish.

For those who like garlic, no roast, sauté, or stew is perfect without one or two cloves of garlic. Very often, garlic is used unpeeled: through its paperlike sheath, garlic can give out its flavour to a sauce or a stock without spoiling it. At the end of the cooking, you can peel the clove, crush it and rub it on some croûtons, or you can use it to thicken sauces which go well with a roast.

Lapin Mariné
Marinated Rabbit

Serves 6. Preparation: 15 min Marinade: 3 hr Cooking: 1 hr 15 min

- ○ 1 1.5kg (3 lb) rabbit, cut into 9 pieces
- ○ 1 bottle dry white wine
- ○ 12 peppercorns
- ○ 3 cloves
- ○ 2 cloves garlic, unpeeled
- ○ 1 bouquet garni: 1 sprig thyme, 2 bay leaves, 6 parsley stalks, 1 sprig tarragon
- ○ salt
- ○ 15ml (1 tbls) flour
- ○ 45ml (3 tbls) oil
- ○ 70g (3 oz) butter

1. 3 hours before cooking the rabbit, prepare the marinade. Pour the wine into a saucepan and add the bouquet garni, cloves, garlic, peppercorns and 2ml (½ tsp) of salt. Bring to the boil and simmer over a low heat for 5 minutes, then remove from the heat and leave to cool.
2. Put the rabbit pieces into a dish and cover with the marinade. Leave to marinate for 3 hours.
3. Drain the rabbit pieces, wipe dry and rub lightly with flour. Strain the marinade through a fine sieve and reserve.
4. Heat the oil in a sauté pan. Add half the butter and brown the rabbit pieces all over.
5. When the rabbit is brown, pour over 100ml (3½ fl oz) of the marinade. When the liquid has evaporated, add the same again and so on until the end of the cooking time (about 1 hour). Turn the rabbit pieces constantly during the cooking.
6. When the rabbit is cooked, tender and golden, place on a serving dish. Put the remaining butter in the sauté pan and incorporate into the cooking juices, beating with a whisk. Pour this sauce (which should be thick) over the rabbit and serve at once.

Chips or sauté potatoes go very well with this dish.

Lapin au Petits Pois
Rabbit with Petits Pois

Serves 4. Preparation: 15 min Cooking: 1 hr 10 min

★

- ○ 1 1.2kg (2½ lb) rabbit, cut into 8 pieces
- ○ 150ml (¼ pint) dry white wine
- ○ 1kg (2½ lb) petits pois
- ○ 12 asparagus tips
- ○ 1 medium-sized onion
- ○ 250g (9 oz) cream
- ○ 30g (1 oz) butter
- ○ 200ml (7 fl oz) water
- ○ 1 sprig tarragon
- ○ salt, pepper and nutmeg

1. Shell the peas. Peel and finely slice the onion. Melt the butter in a flameproof casserole over a very low heat and brown the rabbit pieces. Season. Add the wine and turn the rabbit over a few times, so that the meat absorbs the flavour of the wine.
2. When the wine has completely evaporated, add the onion, asparagus tips, tarragon, peas and a little grated nutmeg. Stir in the cream and add the water. Cover and cook for 1 hour over a very low heat. If there is not enough liquid during the cooking, add a little more water.
3. When the rabbit is cooked, serve hot in the cooking dish.

Fresh herbs, such as parsley, chervil, chives, tarragon, basil and coriander, have such delicate flavours that when they are chopped too finely or in an electric mincer, they tend to loose some of their aromatic qualities. Try not to chop them too finely. When washed and dried on kitchen paper, put the leaves into a glass. Hold the glass in one hand and a pair of scissors in the other, then cut the herbs with the scissors, opening them as widely as the diameter of the glass allows, and turning the glass at the same time. Always chop fresh herbs at the last minute, to retain the maximum flavour.

Lapin au Vinaigre

Serves 6. Preparation: 5 min Marinade: 2 hr Cooking: 1 hr 15 min

Rabbit Marinated and Cooked in Vinegar

★★

○ 1 1.5kg (3½ lb) rabbit, cut into 9 pieces
○ 60ml (4 tbls) wine vinegar
○ 150ml (¼ pint) groundnut oil
○ 3 sprigs thyme
○ 2 bay leaves
○ 5ml (1 tsp) coarse salt

1. 2 hours before cooking the rabbit, put the pieces in an ovenproof dish large enough to lay them flat on the bottom. Pour in the vinegar and turn the pieces over so that the meat is well moistened. Then add the oil and sprinkle in the salt.
2. Cut the sprigs of thyme into 2 and put these pieces in the corners of the dish. Cut the bay leaves into 4 and place them in between the rabbit joints. Marinate for 1 hour. After that time, turn the rabbit pieces over and marinate for another hour.
3. Set the oven to 200°C (400°F; gas mark 6). Cook the rabbit for 1 hour 15 minutes, turning the pieces three or four times during the cooking. Cook for 30 minutes at 200°C (400°F; gas mark 6), 30 minutes at 190°C (375°F; gas mark 5) and 15 minutes at 180°C (350°F; gas mark 4).
4. Serve very hot or cold.

Hot or cold, serve this dish with a green salad, seasoned with herbs and shallots.

Lapin Froid Sauce Piquante

Serves 4. Preparation and cooking: 1 hr 10 min
Marinade: 3 hr

Cold Rabbit with Spicy Sauce

★★

○ 4 rabbit joints, boned
○ 1 onion
○ 1 clove
○ 1 carrot
○ 1 celery stalk
○ 1 bay leaf
○ 10 peppercorns
○ 45ml (3 tbls) white wine vinegar
○ 15ml (1 tbls) coarse salt

For the sauce:
○ 1 small tin tuna in oil
○ 15ml (1 tbls) capers
○ 2 small gherkins (in vinegar)
○ 2 pinches cayenne pepper
○ 4 anchovy fillets
○ 1 small onion
○ the juice of 1 lemon
○ 100ml (3½ fl oz) oil

1. Peel the onion and carrot. Spike the onion with the clove. Remove the threads from the celery stalk.
2. Place the rabbit in a large saucepan, together with the vegetables, bay leaf and peppercorns. Moisten with vinegar and cover with cold water.
3. Cook over a medium heat. When the liquid starts to boil, season with salt and cook for another 40 minutes.
4. Meanwhile, prepare the sauce: chop the capers, gherkins and anchovy fillets. Peel and finely chop the onion. Put the tuna into a bowl and flake it, using a fork, or pound it with a pestle. Add the anchovies, capers, gherkins and onion. Mix well, season with cayenne pepper and pour in the lemon juice. Pour in the oil drop by drop, beating with a fork to fold it into the mixture.
5. After 40 minutes cooking, turn the heat off and remove the rabbit from the casserole, together with the carrot and celery. Drain and leave to cool. Mash the carrot and celery with a fork and mix this purée into the sauce.
6. When the rabbit is cold, cut the flesh into strips and arrange them on a serving dish. Pour the sauce over and leave to marinate for at least 3 hours before serving.

You will find the recipe for civet de lièvre *in many cookery books. Meanwhile, you can prepare* civet de lapin *following the recipe for* coq au vin. *In the case of rabbit, it is imperative to thicken the sauce with the blood of the rabbit.*

Lapin de la Forêt-Noire

Serves 4. Preparation and cooking: 1 hr 30 min

Rabbit in Beer

★★

○ 1 1.2kg (2½ lb) rabbit, cut into 8 pieces
○ 15ml (1 tbls) flour
○ 330ml (½ pint) beer
○ the rabbit liver
○ 3 shallots
○ 1 small celery stalk
○ 60g (2½ oz) butter
○ salt and pepper

1. Dip the rabbit pieces in the flour.
2. Melt half the butter in a flameproof casserole and brown the rabbit all over. Then pour in the beer, season with salt and pepper and cook over a very low heat, uncovered, for 1 hour 20 minutes approximately.
3. 20 minutes before the end of the cooking time, prepare the ingredients for the sauce. Peel and finely chop the shallots. Remove the threads from the celery stalk and chop it finely. Chop up the rabbit liver with a sharp knife.
4. Melt the remaining butter in a frying pan and gently sauté the shallots and celery. Add the liver, stir for 30 seconds, season and turn the heat off.
5. Leave these ingredients to cool, then mince them in an electric mincer or pass them through the fine mesh of a vegetable mill.
6. 5 minutes before the end of the cooking time, add the puréed mixture to the casserole. Mix well and simmer for 5 minutes, turning the rabbit pieces frequently.
7. Serve very hot.

Serve with a smooth purée of potatoes or polenta.

Lapin au Vin Rouge

Serves 4. Preparation and cooking: 1 hr 30 min

Rabbit in Red Wine

★★

○ 1 1.2kg (2½ lb) rabbit, cut into 8 pieces
○ 100g (4 oz) black olives, stoned
○ 2 medium-sized onions
○ 2 cloves garlic
○ 1 bay leaf
○ ¼ litre (9 fl oz) good red wine
○ 1 tin 400g (14 oz) peeled tomatoes
○ 60ml (4 tbls) oil
○ 60g (2 oz) butter
○ 250g (9 oz) button mushrooms
○ 2ml (½ tsp) sugar
○ salt and pepper

1. Peel and finely slice the onions. Crush the cloves of garlic, unpeeled, with the palm of your hand. Sieve the tomatoes or put through the fine mesh of a vegetable mill. Season with sugar.
2. Heat the oil in a sauté pan. Add half the butter and brown the rabbit, onions, garlic, and olives over a very low heat. Then increase the heat and add the wine. Turn the rabbit pieces all the time until the wine has completely evaporated. Pour in the tomato purée, add the bay leaf, season and cover the pan with a lid. Cook for 1 hour over a low heat.
3. Meanwhile, trim the mushrooms. Wash, wipe and cut them into thin strips. Put the remaining butter in a frying pan and sauté the mushrooms. When they have exuded all their juice and are golden, season with salt and pepper and transfer them into the sauté pan together with their cooking fat.
4. After 1 hour, check whether the rabbit is cooked – it should be tender and the meat should come easily off the bones. Then reduce the sauce, which should be of a thick consistency.
5. Pour the contents of the sauté pan into a dish and serve at once.

Serve with potatoes cut into thin strips, sautéed in butter and sprinkled with parsley, chopped herbs and garlic.

Pigeons au Pistou

Serves 4. Preparation and cooking: 1 hr 5 min

Stuffed Pigeons with Pistou Sauce

★★

- ○ 4 pigeons
- ○ 200g (7 oz) larding fat
- ○ 50g (2 oz) butter
- ○ 100ml (3½ fl oz) dry white wine

For the stuffing
- ○ 50g (2 oz) grated Gruyère
- ○ 150g (5 oz) ham
- ○ 30ml (2 tbls) white breadcrumbs
- ○ 30ml (2 tbls) cream
- ○ 5ml (1 tsp) chopped basil
- ○ 5ml (1 tsp) chopped parsley
- ○ 2ml (½ clove) garlic, finely chopped
- ○ 1 egg
- ○ salt and pepper

For the sauce
- ○ 30ml (2 tbls) chopped parsley
- ○ 30ml (2 tbls) chopped basil
- ○ 50g (2 oz) pine kernels or walnuts
- ○ 1 clove garlic
- ○ 60ml (4 tbls) oil
- ○ 30g (1 oz) butter
- ○ salt and pepper

1. Prepare the stuffing: chop the ham finely and put into a bowl. Add the breadcrumbs, cream, basil, parsley, Gruyère and half clove of garlic. Mix well and season. Mix once more and break in the egg. Mix all well together and divide the stuffing into 4 lumps.
2. Fill each pigeon with one quarter of the stuffing. Sew up the vent with a needle and thread. Place a slice of barding fat on the breast of each pigeon and secure with string.
3. Melt the butter in a flameproof casserole and brown the pigeons over a very low heat (to make sure the butter does not burn). Then pour on the wine and cover with a lid. Simmer over a low heat for 30 minutes.
4. While the pigeons are cooking, prepare the pistou sauce. Put all ingredients for the sauce into an electric blender and mix for 2 minutes, or crush all ingredients in a mortar, using a pestle.
5. 10 minutes before the end of cooking time remove the pigeons from the casserole, discard the string and barding fat and put them back into the casserole, breast downwards.
6. When the pigeons are cooked and browned, pour in the pistou, turn the pigeons over a few times in the sauce for 1 minute and remove from the heat. Serve.

Fresh pasta, such as lightly buttered tagliatelle, goes very well with this deliciously flavoured dish. Place the pasta on a serving dish. Arrange the pigeons on top and pour over the sauce. Serve with some grated Gruyère or Parmesan in a bowl.

Pigeons aux Amandes

Serves 4. Preparation and cooking: 1 hr

Pigeons with Almonds

★★

- ○ 4 pigeons
- ○ 200g (7 oz) blanched almonds
- ○ 1kg (2½ lb) onions
- ○ 150g (5 oz) butter
- ○ 1 pinch saffron threads
- ○ 3 pinches cinnamon
- ○ 30ml (2 tbls) chopped parsley
- ○ the juice of ½ lemon
- ○ salt and pepper

1. Peel and finely slice two onions.
2. Put the 2 onions, butter, saffron, salt, a lot of pepper and 3 pinches of cinnamon into a flameproof casserole. Place the pigeons on top of this seasoning and pour in enough water to three-quarters cover them.
3. Cover with a lid and cook over a medium heat for approximately 45 minutes, turning the pigeons a few times.
4. 20 minutes before the end of the cooking time, add the almonds to the casserole. While the pigeons are cooking, peel and finely chop the remaining onions.
5. When the pigeons are cooked and tender, remove from the casserole and keep them warm. Put the onions and parsley into the casserole and cook over a brisk heat, uncovered. When they are nearly cooked, but still a little firm, sprinkle with lemon juice and put the pigeons back into the casserole for 5 minutes. Turn the birds over a few times to warm them up completely and to ensure that they are properly flavoured by the sauce.
6. Serve very hot, covered with the sauce which should be of a smooth, rather thick consistency.

Pigeons Trois Étoiles

Serves 4. Preparation and cooking: 50 min

Pigeons with Truffle in Brandy and Foie Gras Sauce   ★★★

- ○ **4 pigeons**
- ○ **60g (2½ oz) butter**
- ○ **100g (4 oz) foie gras**
- ○ **1 small truffle**
- ○ **60ml (2 fl oz) fine champagne or brandy**
- ○ **¼ litre (9 fl oz) chicken stock**
- ○ **salt and pepper**

For the croûtons:
- ○ **4 slices of white bread**
- ○ **80g (3 oz) butter**

1. Rub the inside of the pigeons with salt and pepper. Cut the truffle into very thin strips.
2. Melt the butter in a flameproof casserole and brown the pigeons over a very low heat. Season with salt and pepper and add 100ml (3½ fl oz) of chicken stock. Cover with a lid and simmer over a low heat for 30 minutes.
3. 10 minutes before the end of the cooking time, prepare the croûtons. Cut the crusts off the bread, melt the butter in a frying pan and gently fry the slices of bread on both sides. Keep warm in a serving dish.
4. When the pigeons are cooked, remove from the casserole and place each one on a slice of bread. Pour the brandy into the casserole together with the remaining chicken stock. Reduce to a third, by boiling the sauce over a brisk heat for 5 minutes.
5. Reduce the heat and stir in the foie gras, little by little, beating with a whisk to mix the ingredients well.
6. When the sauce is smooth, add the truffle strips and pour over the pigeons. Serve immediately.

Pigeons Suaves

Serves 4. Preparation: 10 min Cooking: 55 min

Pigeons in Creamy Sweet Sauce   ★★

- ○ **4 pigeons**
- ○ **200g (7 oz) barding fat**
- ○ **30ml (2 tbls) oil**
- ○ **40g (1½ oz) butter**
- ○ **½ litre (1 pint) dry white wine**
- ○ **4 sage leaves**
- ○ **4 juniper berries**
- ○ **4 mint leaves**
- ○ **1 clove**
- ○ **2 pinches cinnamon**
- ○ **salt, pepper and nutmeg**
- ○ **250g (9 oz) cream**
- ○ **30ml (2 tbls) rum**

1. Rub the inside of the pigeons with salt and pepper. Place some barding fat on each pigeon breast, securing it with a piece of string.
2. Heat the oil in a flameproof casserole. Add the butter and brown the pigeons all over. Add the sage, mint, juniper berries, clove and cinnamon. Stir well and pour on the wine. Season with salt, pepper and grated nutmeg. Cover with a lid and cook over a medium heat for 30 minutes.
3. Remove the pigeons from the casserole. Discard the string and barding fat and put the pigeons back into the casserole. Cook uncovered until the wine evaporates and the pigeon breasts become brown, then pour on the cream and rum and boil for 5 minutes, until the cream takes on a golden colour.
4. When the pigeons are cooked, place on a serving dish and pour the sauce over.

Serve with rice, mixed with peas and lightly buttered.

A fowl which is spit-roasted should be basted with the cooking juices as often as possible. In the dripping pan underneath the fowl you can add salt, pepper, herbs and some white vermouth or port, but only during the last third of cooking time, when the skin of the fowl is crispy and golden. At the last minute, you can add a small glass of whisky, rum or cognac to the liquid and flame the fowl.

All recipes for chicken apply to pigeon, and vice versa; the same goes for guinea fowl and turkey, and also for goose and duck. Goose, turkey and duck have similar stuffings and similar garnishes.

Sauté de Pigeons aux Morilles

Serves 4. Preparation: 10 min Cooking: 45 min

Sautéed Pigeons with Mushrooms

★★

- ○ **4 pigeons, cut into quarters**
- ○ **250g (9 oz) fresh mushrooms**
- ○ **30ml (2 tbls) oil**
- ○ **50g (2 oz) butter**
- ○ **the juice of ½ lemon**
- ○ **250g (9 oz) cream**
- ○ **15ml (1 tbls) fine champagne or brandy**
- ○ **salt and pepper**

1. Trim the mushrooms. Wash under cold running water and drain.
2. Heat the oil in a sauté pan, add the butter and sauté the pigeons until light brown. Then add the mushrooms, sprinkle with the lemon juice, season with salt and pepper and continue cooking until the cooking juices have completely evaporated. Add a third of the cream to the sauté pan. Reduce the sauce to as little as possible, then stir in another third of the cream, turning the pigeon pieces over continuously.
3. When there is a thick golden sauce in the sauté pan, add the remaining cream together with the brandy. Stir well and reduce the sauce by half; remove from heat.
4. Pour the ingredients of the sauté pan onto a serving dish and serve at once.

Pigeons aux Petits Pois

Serves 2. Preparation: 15 min Cooking: 1 hr 10 min

Pigeons with Petits Pois

★★

- ○ **2 pigeons**
- ○ **150g (5 oz) mild cure bacon**
- ○ **1kg (2½ lb) fresh peas**
- ○ **12 small onions**
- ○ **30ml (2 tbls) oil**
- ○ **60g (2½ oz) butter**
- ○ **1 sprig thyme**
- ○ **1 bay leaf**
- ○ **2ml (½ tsp) sugar**
- ○ **salt and pepper**

1. Shell the peas. Peel the onions. Rub the inside of the pigeons with salt and pepper. Cut the bacon into thin strips. Heat the oil in a flameproof casserole and lightly fry the bacon strips. Then remove from the casserole and reserve.
2. Add half the butter in the casserole and fry the onions over a low heat (to prevent the butter from burning) until golden. Then remove the onions, using a slotted spoon and reserve with the bacon.
3. Brown the pigeons all over in the cooking fat, still over a low heat. Then put the bacon and onions back into the casserole. Add the peas, thyme, and bay leaf. Season with sugar, salt and pepper. Pour in 100ml (3½ fl oz) of water, stir well and cover the casserole with a lid. Simmer for 35 to 40 minutes, until the pigeons and peas are tender.
4. When the ingredients are cooked, add the remaining butter and serve in the cooking dish.

When braising a fowl, you should cook it uncovered in a heavy-bottomed casserole (enamelled cast iron, stainless steel or glazed earthenware) because the cooking is done at a low heat which must be constant (whether it is over the stove or in the oven). Theoretically, you should never remove the lid of the casserole, because the meat and vegetables have to cook in their own juices; the steam which is formed condenses under the lid and drips back into the casserole. But it is possible to add a little liquid to the casserole at the beginning of the cooking, such as wine, stock, vermouth, fruit juice, tomato purée, etc. But if the fowl is cooked with vegetables which already contain a lot of water, such as tomatoes or mushrooms, it is unnecessary.

More tips on braising: the casserole should be large enough to contain the fowl easily, so that the cooking juices do not burn. To get a rich, delicately flavoured sauce, cook the fowl with shallots, onions, garlic, carrots, bacon strips, and spices or herbs according to your taste. But all the ingredients must be kept in proportion, so as not to upset the balance of the sauce, otherwise the dish might have too strong a flavour. Keep in mind that in cooking, moderation leads to perfection.

Pigeons au Raisin Muscat

Pigeons with Muscatels

Serves 4. Preparation: 10 min Cooking: 45 min

- ○ **4 pigeons**
- ○ **200g (7 oz) larding fat**
- ○ **30ml (2 tbls) oil**
- ○ **50g (2 oz) butter**
- ○ **¼ litre (9 fl oz) dry white wine**
- ○ **1 sprig thyme**
- ○ **1 bay leaf**
- ○ **30ml (2 tbls) cognac**
- ○ **salt and pepper**
- ○ **1kg (2½ lb) muscat grapes, black or white**

1. Rub the inside of the pigeons with salt and pepper. Put some larding fat on the breast of each pigeon and secure with string. Heat the oil in a flameproof casserole, add the butter and brown the pigeons all over. Season with salt and pepper, add the thyme and bay leaf and pour over the wine. Cover with a lid and simmer over a low heat for 30 minutes.
2. Meanwhile, wash the grapes and remove the pips. Pass 500g (slightly over 1 lb) of the grapes through the fine mesh of a vegetable mill. Strain the juice once more through a fine sieve and reserve.
3. 10 minutes before the end of the cooking time, remove the pigeons from the casserole. Discard the string and larding fat. Put the pigeons back into the casserole breast downwards, so that they can brown.
4. When the pigeons are brown, pour in the grape juice and cognac. When this starts to boil, add the grapes and simmer for 3 minutes, to let them heat up. Then place the pigeons on a serving dish and arrange the rest of the grapes around. Serve immediately.

Pigeons Chasseur

Pigeons Chasseur

Serves 4. Preparation: 15 min Cooking: 45 min

- ○ **4 young pigeons**
- ○ **12 shallots, finely chopped**
- ○ **24 button mushrooms**
- ○ **4 large ripe tomatoes**
- ○ **½ litre (1 pint) dry white wine**
- ○ **1 sprig thyme**
- ○ **½ bay leaf**
- ○ **10ml (2 tsp) coarsely chopped parsley**
- ○ **30ml (2 tbls) oil**
- ○ **30g (1 oz) butter**
- ○ **salt and pepper**

1. Scald the tomatoes in boiling water for 1 minute, then refresh under cold running water. Peel, remove the seeds, mash with a fork and reserve. Trim the mushrooms, wash and drain.
2. Heat the oil in a flameproof casserole, add the butter and brown the pigeons all over, then remove from the heat and fry the shallots.
3. Cut the mushrooms into 4 pieces. Put them into the casserole with the shallots. When they have turned golden, add the tomato purée, simmer for 2 minutes then pour over the wine.
4. When the sauce starts to boil, put the pigeons back into the casserole together with the thyme and bay leaf. Season with salt and pepper, cover with a lid and cook over a low heat for 25 minutes.
5. When the pigeons are cooked, place them on a serving dish and pour over the contents of the casserole. Sprinkle with parsley and serve at once.

Steamed potatoes or rice, lightly buttered, go very well with this dish.

Basil is a herb which is also known as pistou *in France, because it is the main ingredient of* pistou *sauce.*

Do you know how to cook chicken with tarragon (poulet à l'estragon)? *It is a very simple recipe. First sauté a young chicken, whole or jointed, in a mixture of oil and butter. Cook covered for 40 to 50 minutes. Once cooked, keep the chicken warm and deglaze the cooking juices by adding 100ml (3½ fl oz) of dry white wine into the sauté pan. Reduce the sauce by half, then pour in 100ml (3½ fl oz) of water or stock. Bring to the boil and remove from the heat. Away from the heat, add 5ml (1 tsp) coarsely chopped tarragon and the same amount of chervil. Pour this sauce over the chicken and serve. You can use some cream (instead of the wine) to deglaze the cooking juices.*

Wines: the Finishing Touch

Nowadays excellent quality table wines are within the reach of everyone, though you should expect to pay more for a good vintage wine from one of the famous vineyards, such as Nuits-St-Georges or Schloss Johannisberg Riesling. When buying French wine, look for the *Appellation Contrôlée* label, which is a guarantee of quality.

Below is a guide to the wines that go best with certain foods, but there are no absolute *rules* about which wine to serve with what food – in the end it is your palate that must decide. For a large, formal meal, certain wines traditionally follow each other through the menu and you could serve three or even four wines at one meal. In this case, it is usual to serve dry sherry with the soup, dry white wine with the fish course, claret or burgundy with the meat or game and a white dessert wine or medium sweet champagne with the dessert. For cheese, your guests would return to the claret or burgundy. Certain foods kill the flavour of wine and should therefore be avoided if you are planning to serve wine with the meal. Mint sauce, for example, or any salad with a strong vinaigrette dressing, will destroy the taste of the wine.

Remember that red wines are generally served *chambré*, or at room temperature, to bring out the flavour. Draw the cork at least three or four hours before you plan to drink the wine and let the bottle stand in the kitchen or a warm room. (Never be tempted into putting the bottle in hot water or in front of the fire – the flavour will be ruined.) The exception to the *chambré* rule is Beaujolais, which can be served cool – some people even serve it chilled. White or rosé wines are usually served chilled – the easiest way is to put them in the fridge an hour before serving, or plunge them into an ice bucket, if you have one. Champagne should also be served well chilled and is generally brought to the table in an ice bucket.

Wines to Serve with Food

Oysters, shellfish	Chablis, dry Moselle, Champagne
Fried or grilled fish	Dry Graves, Moselle, Hock, Rosé, Blanc de Blanc
Fish with sauces	Riesling, Pouilly-Fuissé, Chablis
Veal, pork or chicken dishes (served simply)	Rosé, Riesling, a light red wine such as Beaujolais
Chicken or pork served with a rich sauce	Claret, Côte de Rhône, Médoc
Rich meat dishes, steaks, game	Red Burgundy, Rioja, Red Chianti
Lamb or duck	Claret, Beaujolais
Desserts and puddings	White Bordeaux, Sauternes, Entre Deux Mers
Cheese	Burgundy, Rioja, Cabernet Sauvignon

This edition published 1992 by Wordsworth Editions Ltd, 8b East Street, Ware, Hertfordshire.

Copyright © Wordsworth Editions Ltd 1992.

Designed by Tony Selina, The Old Goat Graphic Company, London, England.

The publisher has made every reasonable attempt to obtain full clearance of film material, and will make an appropriate payment in the event of any oversight.

ISBN 1-85326-981-6

Printed and bound in Hong Kong by South China Printing Company.